CONTENTS

INTRODUCTION

"There is always something primordial about travelling over water, even for short distances. You get the feeling you shouldn't be there, an impression conveyed not so much by your eyes, ears, nose, palate or the palms of your hands as by your feet which, somewhat strangely, start to act as another sense organ. Water casts doubt on the whole principle of horizontality, especially at night, when its surface seems like cobbled paving .... On water, for example, you don't let your mind wander as you do on dry land: your legs keep you and your resources under constant control, in a constant state of balance as though you were a kind of compass."

Implicit in the words of Joseph Brodsky — Nobel prizewinner for literature — is a superior form of perception, the fascination of a city like Venice, unrivaled among cities built on water, which brings you face-to-face with a fundamental, though much pondered reality: for humankind, made three-quarters of water, being in Venice is like returning to float in the familiar, comforting surroundings of the womb. And this is the simple secret of this enthralling city, for Venice plunges us into our past, carrying us back in time to our distant origins. *"Nobilissima et singolare"* is how Francesco Sansovino very neatly described Venice in his celebrated guidebook, published in 1581. His choice of adjectives summed up the essential characteristics of the city perfectly: noble in terms of ethical and elective affinity, stemming from the good taste of her population; singular, the city's most obvious and indisputable quality given her unique and incomparable urban structure. A lot more could be said about the "differentness" of Venice, particularly considered with respect to artificiality: few cities can claim to have such a close and necessary relationship with man. Venice came into being when men determinedly and skilfully tore her from the lagoon, creating solid land where before there was only mud, sandbanks, islets and water. Nothing could be more singular than her urban layout, developed as a series of *"sestieri"* or wards (San Marco, Castello, Cannaregio, Dorsoduro, San Polo and Santa Croce), separated by the Grand Canal, which winds its way through the city like a snake. The resulting urban structure appears to have grown at random, with twisting canals and *calli* that seemingly imitate the bends of the main thoroughfare. Also unique is the way the narrow streets of Venice are numbered, a system so strange as to bring tourists to the verge of despair.

12 The façade of St. Mark's is the crowning glory of this square, aptly described as "the loveliest drawing room in the world." The mosaics on the basilica change with the light, emanating streaks of gold at midday and creating an aura of romance on nights lit by a full moon.

13 The Grand Canal winds its way across Venice, dividing the city into two. Visible in this photo are the curious coloured poles whose role was both prestigious and functional: essentially a mooring for gondolas, they often bore heraldic insignia and coats of arms, to mark the "parking space" in the waters of the canal that the noble palazzo were entitled to use. Each residence employed its own gondoliers who, on ceremonious occasions, were attired in splendid livery: silk jacket, knee breeches, red cap and scarf.

Physical contact is unavoidable in Venice. Nobody ever feels alone here: as soon as you step onto the street, you are instantly confronted and engulfed by every imaginable manifestation of civilized society (and, inevitably, with occasional evidence of incivility too.)

Time has a different dimension in Venice. Her clocks seem to stand still, leaving you caught for a moment in some kind of spell, detached from reality, change, aging. Eternity is a dimension that suits Venice well, part and parcel of her own special brand of real

life. As soon as you step onto a gondola or one of her funny little water-buses, you realize that time passes more slowly here: even the shortest journey takes far longer than in any other city of the world. It is as though amenities like transport have learned to conform with the slowed-down pace of time. And yet what shapes life here is an ever-present dualism, the clash between this unsuppressable idea of timelessness and an ominous sense of ephemerality that soon rears its ugly head. For Venice is a fragile city: high water, a sudden heavy shower of rain, a few inches of snow, and chaos ensues. Eternity and fragility cohabit like love and death in a tender embrace romantically immortalized by poets and writers through the ages. Eros and

Thanatos, love and death. How many lovers have seen their passion blossom and die in Venice! In Venice every manifestation of nature is seen in a totally different light. As the sun sinks into the vast, still waters of the lagoon, radiating flashes of fire, each sunset is cloaked in a portentous sadness, *"désespoir d'une beauté qui s'en va vers la mort"*: "The horizontal light of evening sets Venice aflame, embellishing the Punta della Dogana and the church of La Salute (which, all things told, is a most mediocre building), and the sun works its magic on the canals which instead give off foul smells. Many times, at this hour, I heard the music of the Venice Carnival, those nostalgic arias that echo from one generation to the next, and I saw the great shadowy figures who give momentum to those flat spaces. They raced like clouds, on closer examination they were clouds; for they are the very essence, the solid core of Venice, which preys on the predispositions of its esteemed visitors. As the sound of Ave Marias rings out across Venice, the shadows that rise and fall on the Adriatic sunset weigh heavily on the spirit." Venice is a strange city! Her entire existence is conditioned by the dualism rooted in her soul, every aspect of the city helps create her magic: joy and sadness, meeting and separation, chaste love and licentious, sacred and profane.... But, as Jean Cocteau wrote, "this is a city where pigeons walk and lions fly, so what else should we expect?"

14-15 Venice Carnival is one of the city's biggest tourist attractions, though it has existed in its present form since 1980, when the Biennale organized an event entitled Carnevale del Teatro, under the memorable direction of Maurizio Scaparro. Sad to say, the cultural content of the Carnival declines each year, and the festivities are now an easily forgotten caprice, a typical manifestation of our consumer society.

16-17 This splendid aerial photo of Venice highlights its intriguing shape, like a fish serenely afloat in its natural habitat. An intricate maze of streets, alleyways, squares, marketplaces on either side of the upturned "S" that divides the city in two. This city planning conveys the greatness of the Venetian people who battled against

nature and succeeded in building a city out of a desolate marshland formed of ephemeral islets, shifting sands and water.

18-19 The handsome Benedictine complex of San Giorgio Maggiore in St. Mark's Basin is profiled in the light of the setting sun as the sky slowly turns from red to shades of purple. Through the centuries imposing buildings designed by the architects Palladio, Scamozzi, and Longhena have added to the splendour of the "island of cypresses," as it was once called. Since 1951 the island has hosted the Fondazione Giorgio Cini, the city's foremost international cultural centre for science, fine arts and the humanities.

CANALE DI CANNAREGIO

PORT

RAILWAY STATION

GRAND CANAL

PIAZZALE ROMA

ISLAND OF SACCA FISOLA

DOG

CHUR
SANTA M

ACCADEMIA BRIDGE

CHURCH OF IL RED

ISLAND OF SACCA SAN BIAGIO

ISLAND OF GIUDECCA

RIALTO BRIDGE

ISLAND OF SAN MICHELE (CEMETERY)

CHURCH OF SAN GIOVANNI E PAOLO

BRIDGE OF SIGHS
DOGES' PALACE

BACINO
DELL'ARSENALE

DELLA
A MAR

ST. MARK'S BASILICA

RIVA DEGLI SCHIAVONI

ST. MARK'S SQUARE

DELLA SALUTE

CHURCH OF
LE ZITELLE

BIENNALE ART EXHIBITION

RE

ISLAND OF
SAN GIORGIO
MAGGIORE

ISLAND OF SANT'ELENA

RISE AND FALL OF THE SERENISSIMA: THE HISTORY OF VENICE

No amazing legends surround the origins of Venice, no illustrious figures of antiquity are attributed with founding the city. The last Trojans had been appropriated by imperial Rome and nearby Padua; the gods and mythical heroes who populate the lofty heights of Olympus are notable only for their absence. For the small archipelago of islands in the lagoon no venerable patriarch was invented: the descendants of the first Venetians refused to embellish the history of their city with some borrowed myth or legend. The beauty of her unique, uplifting panorama was more than adequate compensation. Moreover, the fact of her creation from nothing added grist to the mill of the Venetians' immutable independence, an enviable quality that the Most Serene Republic was to boast of for many centuries. The city that emerged from the sea — as D'Annunzio delighted in defining Venice — could be likened only to Aphrodite, goddess of love and beauty, born from the foam of the ocean waves. Continuous, sweeping and unhaltable raids by barbarians on the nearby mainland forced the populations of towns and villages to seek safer refuge among the islets and sandbanks of the lagoon. Only Attila, "Scourge of God," gets a personal mention in tales of the city's origins: the huge stone seat still to be seen in the piazza of Torcella is, by tradition, attributed to the leader of the Huns. Just as unlikely are reports of treasures buried on islets dotted about the lagoon, or the very precise — and hence highly improbable — date of March 25, 421, given as the formal foundation of the city, after the devastating passage of Alaric and his descendants, leaders of the Visigoths. More realistic pages of history tell us instead how the process whereby mainland Venice became maritime Venice was primarily linked to the threat of a Lombard invasion. For the Lombards who swept across Byzantine Italy in the second half of the sixth century had different motives from the previous barbarian invaders: having conquered these lands, they intended to stay. The earliest description of the lagoon and the life of its inhabitants is found in a letter written by Flavius Magnus Aurelius Cassiodorus, an official at the court of the Ostrogoths in 537–538; in it he urges the "maritime tribunes" to arrange for the transportation of foodstuffs from Istria to Ravenna. Reading between the lines (the letter abounds in the pompous rhetoric typical of that time), a picture emerges of a simple existence, based on fishing and trading salt gathered from the marshes; houses scattered about the lagoon, built on embankments surrounded by barriers formed of wattle and osier, like the nests of seabirds, some firmly rooted to dry land, others confidently afloat; and boats without sails or oars, but pulled across the water with ropes. The scene evoked has an undeniable resemblance to a "republic of beavers," as Venice was to be defined

20 top The woodcut by Reuwich of which we see a detail here was made to illustrate the book by Bernard von Breydenbach in which the author tells the story of his pilgrimage from Mainz to the Holy Land in the second half of the 1400s.
This fairly faithful view — one of the oldest in existence — shows Venice from the island of San Giorgio, a viewpoint used for many etchings of later centuries.

20-21 One of Vittore Carpaccio's last works, conserved in the Doges' Palace and dated 1516, is an emblematic portrayal of the dominion of Venice over land and sea, based on the symbol of the Serenissima.

The winged lion is shown with its right front paw placed on the Gospel, and the left one resting firmly on the ground; the back paws are, as if by magic, resting on water.
In the background

to the left is St. Mark's Basin with the Doges' Palace, the Campanile, the Piazzetta, and Molo; visible on the right, behind Venetian ships with sails billowing in the wind, is San Nicol di Lido.

21 bottom Another luminous veduta of the Doges' Palace from St. Mark's Basin, its waters thronging with barges and graceful gondolas with felze hardtops.

The vivacious atmospheric effects are created by Francesco Guardi's rich palette of colour (the painting is in the National Gallery, London).

22 top This important
16th-century
manuscript by
Cristoforo Sabbadino
— which can be seen
in the Biblioteca
Nazionale Marciana

in Venice — offers a
graphically simple
but nonetheless
effective impression
of the first settlements
in the Venetian
lagoon.

22 bottom Although
Paolo Veneziano is
considered a member
of the neo-Hellenist
movement, the last
phase of the
Byzantine tradition,
he has his own
distinctive style, as is
evident from this
detail of his Pala
feriale di San Marco
(1345), exhibited in

St. Mark's Museum
(it depicts the altar-
frontal used to cover
the Pala d'Oro on
weekdays).
The innovative
elements of the
painting are its use
of colour and
amazing vibrancy,
stylistic trademarks
of this 14th-century
Venetian artist.

many centuries later (on September 28, 1786) by an authoritative traveller, Johann Wolfgang von Goethe. The effects of the Lombard invasion (568) were soon felt on the mainland and the populations who had pinned their hopes of survival on the tiny islands of the lagoon initially looked East to the Byzantine Empire for protection, focusing their interests on the sea and ships. As Venice grew, she slowly freed herself from the grip of Byzantine sovereignty, with a duke appointed directly by her own people. The community's seat of government was sited first on Malamocco (742) and later on the more central Rialtine islands (810), historic core of the Venice of future centuries. Around that time the Franks also arrived in the area, called by the pope to help fight the Lombards. After the Frankish conquest of the Lombard kingdom, Venice witnessed another bloodbath between Byzantines and Franks: Pepin's flotilla came uncomfortably close but — as fortune had it — ran aground on the shoals and shallows of the lagoon. The city was saved, as was the new seat of government at Rivoalto (Rialto), and Venice was well set on her way to becoming a small state. All she now needed was a tutelary saint: needless to say, for a city that made no secret of her ambitions, the Byzantine St. Theodore was considered over-endowed with humility and definitely short on charisma. As saints were in rather limited supply, the Venetians decided they could do no better

than go and steal one. Which explains how, in 828, with the aid of Venetian merchants, the mortal remains of Mark the Evangelist were brought from Alexandria, in Egypt, to the lagoon. In later years, the Venetians even had the audacity to justify their action — probably best qualified as body-snatching — by saying it was no more than fulfillment of the last will and testimony of the Evangelist himself. But why should we be shocked at this strange confusion of the sacred and profane, when even the Greeks honoured Hermes as the deity of gain, both honest and dishonest? But this is the point where the real story of the Most Serene Republic starts, and a compendium of the most significant dates and events in its history is offered in these pages. An event now cloaked in legend occurred around 946 – 948, although it would hardly be realistic to give a precise date to the kidnapping of young Venetian brides. The episode is closely linked with Venice's early years as a trading power, when she very soon had to contend with piracy from the Slavs. Fearful pirates who had their lairs around the mouths of the Narenta River (now better known by the Slavonic name of Neretva) were responsible for this famous act of aggression. But the Venetians succeeded in rescuing their brides, and the victory was celebrated with a "mass" wedding, now commemorated as the Festa delle Marie (the Feast-Day of the Daughters of the Virgin).

VENETIAE CONDITA
CIVITAS ANNO
ADMIRABILIS A·SALVTE
POST·EVERSAM HOMINIBVS
AB·ATTILA RESTITVTA
HVNNOR·REGE CCCCLIIII
AQVILEIAM

23 Few cities can boast such an enormous range of bird's-eye views as Venice: from views printed towards the end of the 1400s — culminating in Jacopo de Barbari's splendid work of 1500 — to the products of increasingly advanced technology, most recently exemplified by the huge vertical aerial photograph of 1985, produced with the collaboration of the City Council's Urban Planning Department.

24 top Enrico Dandolo was already an old man when he was appointed doge (according to tradition, an octogenarian, but still in excellent physical shape). But during his short rule (1192 –1205) he brought to fruition an amazing scheme: he succeeded in exploiting a Crusade for the purposes of his city. Remembered by the Venetians as "more imperial than the emperor," he died in Constantinople and was buried there in the church of St. Sofia.

I n the tenth and eleventh centuries Venice consolidated her supremacy in the Adriatic. The Emperor of Byzantium allowed Venetian merchants to pay preferential tariffs. The struggle to subdue pirates, Normans and Saracens and defend the trade routes of the Adriatic continued and was intensified. Around the year 1000 the Venetian fleet, under the command of doge Pietro Orseolo II, journeyed down the coast of Dalmatia, where cities and towns agreed to accept the protection of the Republic. Venice thus began to extend her control over the Adriatic Sea, laying solid foundations for her imperial future. The city now needed a demonstration of her power that would also highlight her political and artistic prestige. In 1094 St. Mark's Basilica was consecrated; just a few years later, reportedly in 1104, work began on building the initial core of the Arsenal. The culminating moment for the burgeoning city-republic came in 1177 when, thanks to skilful diplomatic manoeuvres, Venice was ready to act as host for the reconciliation of pope and emperor. Having completed urban and architectural renovation schemes, including the new square in front of St. Mark's, the city triumphantly welcomed the meeting between Pope Alexander III and Emperor Frederick Barbarossa. To mark the occasion the pope offered the doge a gift: a ring subsequently used for the Marriage to the Sea, the ceremony that symbolically established

24 centre The four gilded bronze horses of St. Mark were brought to Venice in 1204 among the spoils of the Fourth Crusade. They had stood in the hippodrome of Constantinople and miraculously survived the fire started during the seige of the city. After careful restoration, the original horses are now in St. Mark's Museum: the ones high up on the gallery of the basilica are only copies.

24 bottom A group of statues in porphyry, of 4th-century Syrian origin — known as the Tetrarchs — stands at the southern corner of the Treasury of St. Mark, close to the Doges' Palace.

The emperor Diocletian is portrayed with his "imperial colleagues," the figures clasped in an embrace symbolizing the unity of the Roman Empire.

24-25 The Sack of Constantinople, *Domenico Tintoretto's huge painting, in the Sala del Maggior Consiglio (Great Council Chamber), depicts the conquest of Constantinople, which took place after the old doge Enrico* Dandolo decided on *a change of plan for the armies of the Fourth Crusade. Thanks to its success, he acquired the title of Lord and Master of a Quarter and a Half-Quarter of the Eastern Roman Empire.*

25 top The Treasury of St. Mark is a precious collection of liturgical objects and reliquaries. Most of them arrived in Venice as spoils from the conquest of Constantinople. One of the most beautiful pieces is an icon of the Archangel Michael, worked in relief on embossed gold leaf by 10th-century Byzantine goldsmiths.

26 top *This is how, in the 1700s, Giovanni Grevembroch imagined the clothes worn by* Marco Polo *in Tartary, in a watercolor from his Venetian costumes series.*

26 bottom *The doges of the Serenissima are portrayed in the frieze around the walls of the Great Council Chamber, in the Doges' Palace. After Andrea Dandolo's portrait, in the place of Marin Faliero's (1354–1355), condemned to death for conspiring against the Republic, a somber black veil reads:* "Hic est locus Marini Faletri decapitati pro criminibus."

Venice's supremacy over the waters of the Adriatic. The maritime republics were by now firmly set on their upward path. Transporting crusaders to the Holy Land provided them with a source of revenue. In 1201–1204 Venice took part in the Fourth Crusade, upon being contracted to provide ships to transport the knights of the Crusade and their supporting army. In spite of his age and blindness, doge Enrico Dandolo was a man of great intuition: instead of demanding payment, he asked for assistance in recapturing the city of Zara and, subsequently, demanded the sack of Constantinople. By the terms of the treaty with the Crusaders, Venice eventually became mistress of "a quarter and half a quarter" of the city and East Roman Empire, acquiring dominion over part of Constantinople and many islands and ports of Greece. The most significant of the many treasures pillaged and plundered during the expedition were the four bronze horses later to decorate the façade of St. Mark's. In 1295 Marco Polo returned to Venice, having lived through amazing experiences related in *Il Milione*, the story of his adventures and travels. Towards the end of the thirteenth century the question of control in the East led to further wars with the rival republic of Genoa (1294–1299). Meanwhile, new tensions and struggles exploded on the home front with the Serrata — literally, the locking — del Maggior Consiglio in 1297: the right to participate in the sessions of the Great Council was limited to an inner elite, members of patrician families who had sat on the Council for the four previous years. Now an "aristocratic" republic and a hereditary oligarchy, fourteenth-century Venice had to ward off several attempts to overthrow her government: the first occurred in 1310, with a conspiracy plotted by Baimonte Tiepolo, Marco Querini and Badoero Badoer. The most lasting imprint of this failed insurrection and averted danger was the institution of the feared Council of Ten, a body set up to watch over the security of the State and to repress any signs of unrest or rebellion. Venice survived the terrible Black Death of 1348, brought to the city by merchant ships carrying goods from the Black Sea, but the republic was soon to experience another serious threat: in 1355 doge Marino Falier made an unsuccessful attempt to overthrow the government and was beheaded for his crime. In the Chamber of the Great Council, along the frieze of ducal portraits, his likeness was removed and replaced with a black veil.

28 top In another small detail from the left side of Gentile Bellini's huge painting we see a priest holding music and others intoning solemn liturgical chants to accompany the procession.

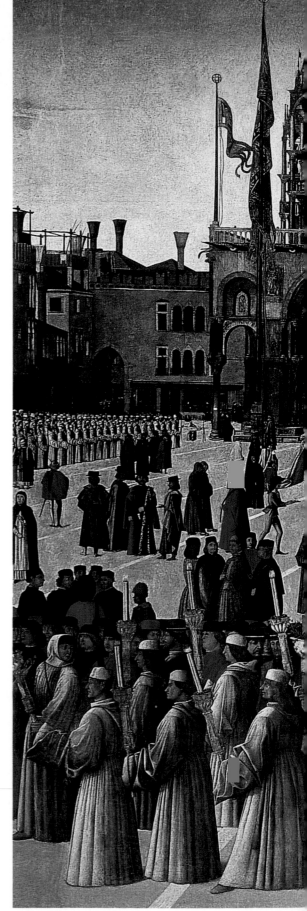

The republics of Venice and Genoa had both become powerful as a result of the crusades and their trade dealings with the Byzantine and Arab worlds, and the war between them grew more intense (1378–1381) as each struggled to gain control of trade with the East. Things came to a head when Genoa almost succeeded in taking Chioggia (1379); a peace conference in Turin brought hostilities to an end but, for Genoa, marked the start of a slow but inexorable decline. During the first three decades of the fifteenth century Venice turned her attention to the Italian mainland and began to extend her territories. Many cities agreed to accept the protection of the standard of St. Mark or were forced into submission: Treviso, Padua, Vicenza, Verona, Belluno, Feltre, Cividale, Udine, Brescia, Bergamo. Further conquest in mainland Italy — in keeping with the imperialist policy of doge Francesco Foscari — brought Milan under Venetian control. But in the second half of the century a new obstacle stood in the way of her territorial ambitions: the Ottoman Empire. In 1453 the Turks took Constantinople. Venice, meanwhile, began to lose some of her lands, among them Negropont. The acquisition of one important strategic base was but small compensation for the many losses suffered: in 1489, Caterina Cornaro, widow of James of Lusignan and queen of Cyprus, returned to Venice, where she abdicated and formally ceded the island to the Serenissima. France and Spain had again changed the balance of power on the European scenario and both kingdoms looked towards Italy with unconcealed interest. In view of Venice's reluctance to return the cities of Romagna she had occupied after the death of Cesare Borgia, Pope Julius II decided — in 1508 — to form a league against the Serenissima with Louis XII of France, Maximilian of Austria, Ferdinand of Aragon and several Italian states.

The League of Cambrai, promoted by the pope, obtained the support he was looking for: France, Spain and the Empire were enthusiastically united in their desire to share-out the territories of the Serenissima. The Venetian mainland was invaded and the republic suffered a crushing defeat at Agnadello. And new dangers for Venice were spelled out by the election to the imperial throne of Charles V of Spain, ruler of the Netherlands, the kingdom of Naples and Austrian territories. And yet during this period Venice became a leading centre of art and culture, thanks in part to its important printing works; it was an ethnic melting pot with large communities of Albanians, Greeks, Armenians, Germans and Jews; it was also the European capital of high life, prodigality, gaiety and licentiousness.

30 top As early as the 13th century, the Serenissima set up a weapons store in the Doges' Palace, to be ready for any eventuality and defend the state against possible attack. Today the Sale d'armi (Arms Rooms) contain museum pieces of exceptional historic value and emblematic of the republic's glorious past. One of the items conserved in this armory is a Turkish buckler, a shield richly decorated with Oriental motifs.

30-31 The battle of Lepanto, on October 7, 1571, was one of the most important moments in the history of the Most Serene Republic, when the Christian alliance routed the Ottoman fleet once and for all. This overwhelming victory is immortalized in grandiose style in a painting by Andrea Vicentino, in the Sala dello Scrutinio (Vote Counting Chamber) of the Doges' Palace.

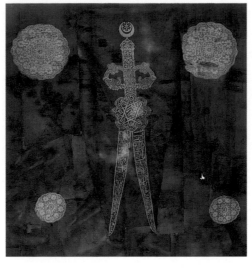

In 1516 the Jews of Venice were confined to the Ghetto Novo, a fortress-like complex on the site of an abandoned foundry. The term ghetto — sadly destined to enter common usage — derives from the Venetian word *ghetto* (meaning cast or casting), namely the foundries where metal to build cannons had once been cast. The problems of the Most Serene Republic were, however, far from over. New storm clouds were gathering on the horizon and threatening its colonies: in 1571 the Turks conquered Cyprus. The Christian army, under the banner of the League, sent its fleet to meet the Turkish foe and on October 7, 1571, the Turks were overwhelmed in a memorable battle at Lepanto, in which Sebastiano Venier, the captain-general of the Venetians, distinguished himself for his bravery. Only a few years later, in 1575–76, a terrible plague struck Venice and brought the city virtually to her knees.

With the last years of the sixteenth century Venice began to decline into economic stagnation as a consequence of the new Atlantic routes and new trade frontiers opened up by Dutch and English ships. Venice was also increasingly harassed by the Turks, by the threat their advance posed for its possessions in the Aegean.

31 top A flag captured from the Ottoman Turks during the bloody battle of Lepanto is now displayed in the Museo Civico Correr.

31 bottom The photo shows a bronze bust of the commander Sebastiano Venier by sculptor Tiziano Aspetti.

32-33 *The Turks were constantly harassing Venetian colonies in the Eastern Mediterranean and for centuries they were the Republic's fiercest enemies. Every victory scored against them was immortalized in huge paintings in the Doges' Palace, for instance this* Victory of the Venetians Over the Turks in the Dardanelles, Under the Command of Lorenzo Marcello *(1656). The picture, by Pietro Liberi, is famous mainly for the giant-like figure at the bottom, portrayed in the act of striking a Turk and commonly known as Libero's Slave.*

The seventeenth century was interspersed with a long series of negative events. In 1606 the Republic refused to hand over to the ecclesiastical authorities two clerics found guilty of common crimes; Pope Paul V responded with an interdict against the city of Venice, that continued to defend "reasons of State" against the increasingly frequent interference of the Roman Curia. Paolo Sarpi, the theologist and advocate of the Republic, defended the rights of the State and was excommunicated. A year later he was the victim of a knife attack. In 1618 a conspiracy against the Serenissima, plotted by Spain, was foiled in the nick of time and its participants fittingly liquidated. While, in 1630, a fierce war was being waged in the Marquisate of Montferrat in defence of the ruling dukes of Mantua, Venice also had to cope with the forays of Uskok pirates, financed by the archduke of Austria. The city was again afflicted by a terrible pestilence, which lasted almost 16 months and claimed nearly a third of the population. As a prayer for deliverance, the Venetians solemnly promised to build a sanctuary to the Virgin. When the epidemic was at last over, they kept their word: the church of Saint Maria della Salute was built, to the plans of architect Baldassare Longhena.

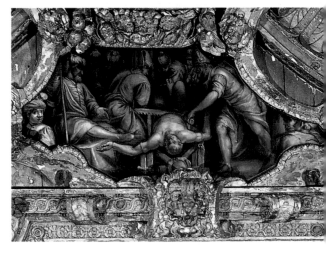

32 bottom Departure of Morosini for the Near East, *Museo Correr.* The fall of Crete (1669) had, in a way, signaled the end of the Serenissima's heyday as a maritime power in the Eastern Mediterranean. But Francesco Morosini gave a new boost to *its military prowess with the conquest of the Morea, i.e. Peloponnese. His name and reputation were sadly darkened forever when, during the capture of Athens, mortar fire hit the Parthenon, used by the Turks as a powder magazine.*

33 In two minor sections of the ceiling of the Sala del Maggior Consiglio are two monochrome paintings of historic interest. They depict episodes of heroism by Venetians defending the city's conquests in the Near East against the Turks, who are shown here at their most cruel. The picture below shows the commander Armario sawn in two by the Turks. Above is Marcantonio Bragadin, valiant defender of Famagosta; after the city fell, he was cruelly punished for what his enemy considered excessive arrogance. His nose and ears were cut off and, a few days later, he was flayed alive.

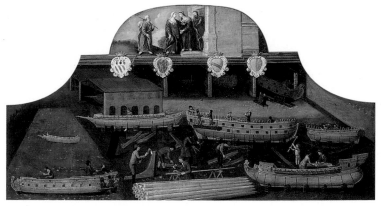

To halt the terrifying advance of the Turks in 1645 Venice began a tremendous war in defence of Crete — or, as the Venetians called it after its capital city, Candia. The war dragged on until 1669 but the island was lost forever. With the coffers of the Republic left disturbingly empty by the war effort, it was agreed that, upon payment of 100,000 ducats, a number of families would be allowed to join the Great Council, i.e., they would be admitted to the ranks of the nobility, with registration in the Golden Book of patrician marriages and births. As the seventeenth century entered its penultimate decade, some ray of hope appeared on the Venetian horizon. The Polish King John Sobieski defeated the Turks who were holding Vienna to siege. Venice formed an alliance with Austria and Russia, and thanks to the skill of her captain-general, Francesco Morosini, the Morea (Peloponnese) was liberated in the space of only two years (1685–1687). The Treaty of Karlowitz (1699) ratified Venetian possession of the territories of the Morea. The joy of Venice was short-lived, however, for by 1718 the Turks had already reconquered the Morea. In the Treaty of Passarowitz this situation was acknowledged and the frontiers of the Venetian Empire were drawn for the last time, for there were to be no further gains or losses. Even with a policy of neutrality, Venice had to be armed and this further drain on its already virtually exhausted coffers set the Republic moving even

faster on the downhill path to economic decline. But among members of the international beau monde, Venice enjoyed new success as the capital of debauchery, gambling, entertainment and everlasting Carnival. The city became a fundamental "port of call" on the grand tour of Europe, the de rigueur destination for enlightened travellers anxious to enhance their cultural development. Venice was the city of theatre, culture and art, of Carlo Goldoni and the Gozzi brothers, of Guardi and Canaletto, of the celebrated Ospedali-Conservatori, centres of music renowned throughout Europe, where Antonio Vivaldi was a teacher and Benedetto Marcello and Tomaso Albinoni contributed their outstanding artistic talents. In 1744 work started on a colossal undertaking, the construction of the Murazzi, gigantic sea-walls stretching along the lagoon littoral between Pellestrina and Chioggia. Although the decline of the Serenissima was increasingly evident, the "show" had to go on: it was necessary to prove to the rest of the world that the queen of the Adriatic continued to reign, even if much of her gloss had disappeared while wars drained her energies and resources. An important opportunity came in 1782 when the visiting grand duke and duchess of Russia — travelling as the Count and Countess of the North — were received with all honours, in the very grandest style. The end was approaching; in 1785 a lodge of Freemasons was discovered.

34-35 and 34 bottom The Marriage to the Sea was among the most loved festivities. Every year on Ascension Day the doge was carried to the port of the Lido in the bucentaur, the gilded state barge. Here the doge threw his ring into the water, accompanied by a colourful procession of boats. Two moments of this ceremony are portrayed in works by two great Venetian painters: The Return of the Bucentaur to the Molo on Ascension Day *by Antonio Canal, known as Canaletto (below, Royal Collection, Windsor Castle); and* Departure of the Bucentaur on Ascension Day *by Francesco Guardi (above, in the Louvre).*

35 The sign of the Guild of Shipwrights was painted by an anonymous artist in 1517. It shows the many kinds of craft work done by the carpenters who specialized in the construction of ships, who worked in the Arsenal and in the squeri.

36-37 *The Venetian custom of setting up bull chases as part of the Carnival festivities — turning "genteel" Venice into a small-scale Pamplona — has remote origins. The* Bull Chase in Campo San Polo *by Heintz the Younger — conserved in the Museo Correr — offers a fine example of this traditional event.*

36 top *In 1782 musical entertainment was arranged in honour of the visiting Count and Countess of the North,* the grand duke of Russia, Paul Petrovich, *and his wife, in the Casino dei Filarmonici, by the church of San Geminiano, near the Procuratie Nuove.*

It took the form most appreciated by foreign guests: a cantata sung by 80 orphan girls from the city's four main charitable institutions. It was an exceptional musical event, immortalized in this painting by Gabriel Bella, in the Pinacoteca Querini Stampalia.

Venice knew other powers were plotting her demise. The new developments in France confirmed her fears. The war spread into Italy too, and the triumphant armies of Napoleon offered a foretaste of what was to come. On April 20, 1797 a French lugger entered the port of Venice Lido, in spite of warnings. A Venetian ship rammed the enemy vessel. The French representative in Venice lodged a formal protest and asked for reparations and for the arrest of the Venetian commander responsible for the disastrous incident. Napoleon's armies were by then at the gates of the city; on May 12, the Great Council voted to accept the constitutional changes proposed by Bonaparte.

The Serenissima was doomed. On May 16, French troops entered Venice. On October 17, the Treaty of Campo Formio was signed and Venice was handed over to Austria.

After a thousand years, the story of the Most Serene Republic had thus come to an end and a period of foreign domination began. Amazed and saddened, the Venetians watched as their city was passed back and forth between France and Austria: after the first period of Austrian domination (1798–1805), with the Treaty of Pressburg, Venice was returned to French rule as part of the Napoleonic Kingdom of Italy (1805–1814).

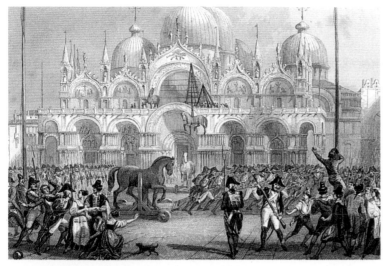

38 top left During their occupation of Venice the French carried off numerous works of art. Not even the four bronze horses of St. Mark were spared: in 1797 they were shipped off to Paris to adorn the entrance to the Tuileries Gardens. This engraving shows French soldiers trying to curb the furious protests of the Venetians as they watched their city being plundered. The horses were brought back to Venice on December 13, 1815. The artist Antonio Canova is said to have played a major part in obtaining their return.

38 top right On March 17, 1848, tricolor flags were hoisted on the flagpoles in St. Mark's Square and the first outbreaks of violence occurred. Quadri's Caf, a favourite haunt of Austrian officers, was devastated. This print shows the scene the next morning, when the Venetians started to attack in earnest. They pulled up paving stones and used them as "ammunition." On March 22, the whole population rose up against the Austrians, forcing them to surrender and withdraw from the city. A provisional government was formed, led by Daniele Manin.

38-39 This tempera painting by Querena (in the Museo del Risorgimento e dell'Ottocento Veneziano) shows St. Mark's Square on March 22, 1848, as the liberated people of Venice hoisted the tricolor flags.

39 bottom Several iron bridges were built during the period of Austrian rule. Shown in this 19th-century lithographic print is the Accademia Bridge, designed by Alfred Henry Neville and inaugurated on November 20, 1854. Standing in its place today is a typical wooden bridge.

Napoleon's definitive downfall marked the start of the second period of Austrian rule (1814–1848). During these years the face of Venice changed. Extensive economic intervention was accompanied by much more noticeable changes to the urban scenario with demolitions, restructuring, new gardens and lost insularity, a consequence of the causeway built, in 1841–46, to bring the railway across the lagoon. A Venetian poet lamented this catastrophe with two wistful lines: "The lagoon is turned into mainland, Venice laughs and I weep at her folly."

After the tumultuous uprising against Austria in 1848–49 a republican government was set up but it lasted for only five brave months before being forced to capitulate on August 24, 1849.

The Austrians returned and stayed put until 1866. For centuries only one bridge — the Ponte di Rialto — had crossed the Grand Canal; between 1854 and 1858 two new cast-iron bridges were built: the Ponte dell'Accademia and the railway station bridge. In 1857 Giovanni Busetto, nicknamed Fisola, opened the first bathing establishment at the Lido, and high-society tourists again made the pearl of the Adriatic one of their favorite destinations. In 1866, by popular vote, Venice was incorporated into the Kingdom of Italy.

With Venice now part of Italy, general restructuring — including changes to urban layout and facilities — continued apace, amid fierce argument. Palazzi, cafés once haunted by literati, bridges and ferries disappeared; roads were built; and improvements made to the city's port, which moved from St. Mark's Basin to the new Stazione Marittima. The old houses of fishermen in working-class districts were demolished and the city skyline was changed by the soaring chimneys of new factories. As though to compensate for these concessions to the dictates of the modern world, Venice prepared to assume a new role as a capital of culture, with the International Art Exhibition of 1895.

Early in the new century (1902) came a sorry episode: the collapse of St. Mark's Campanile, the world's most famous bell-tower, was almost a foretaste of the devastation that wars had yet to bring. The campanile was nevertheless rapidly rebuilt "as was," on its former site. The city withstood the onslaught of the bloodiest of wars, where possible protecting her treasures with shoring and sandbags. But the bombing raids by Austrian planes did not spare either civilian targets or the splendid monuments of this jewel of a city. Hundreds of bombs — in all some 32,400 pounds of explosives — were dropped on Venice. Next came the development of the new industrial zone and port of Marghera (1917); the 1920s and Venice of the Fascist era, with waving banners, muskets, marching children of the Fascist paramilitary youth movements parading before party officials in uniform; *Il Duce* and Hitler celebrating their first pact before thronging crowds in St. Mark's Square. Before long Venice returned to the cultural limelight, with important international events: the first Venice Film Festival was inaugurated on August 6, 1932. At the Theatre Festival, held in 1934, plays set in Venice were performed in the open air, in their "natural" surroundings: Shakespeare's *The Merchant of Venice*, directed by Max Reinhardt and staged in Campo di San Trovaso, was a resounding success. Soon grim scenes of war again invaded Venice, littering her *campi* and streets with ugly dome-shaped air-raid shelters. The partisan uprising and liberation from the Nazis and Fascists are among the closing events of this compendium of the city's history. From the postwar years to the present day, Venice has experienced increasingly frequent flooding: the flood of November 4, 1966 had devastating results. *Acqua alta* and a plethora of other problems are, little by little, destroying this magical city.

40 The collapse of the Campanile, in a period photographic reconstruction of the event. On the morning of July 14, 1902, a crack in the Campanile widened and the Paron de casa, the world's best known bell-tower, suddenly subsided to the ground, leaving an enormous mound of dust and rubble at its base. It happened at 9:52 a.m. Fortunately, no one was hurt as there had been unmistakable signs of the imminent disaster and the area had been cordoned off and cleared. That very same evening the mayor, Filippo Grimani, called a meeting of the city council, and it was unanimously voted to rebuild the Campanile, copying the original down to the most minute detail. And on April 25, 1912, the new Campanile was inaugurated, with a grand ceremony.

40-41 This old photo offers a fine view of St. Mark's Square, with the tricolor hanging from the three flagpoles, supported by bronze bases made by Alessandro Leopardi in 1505. At the time of the Serenissima, only the glorious banner of St. Mark fluttered at the top of the poles.

41 bottom left On the morning of April 30, 1895, a cheering crowd greeted Umberto I and Margherita of Savoy during their visit to Venice to inaugurate the International Art Exhibition, the first edition of the Biennale, a success story that continues today.

41 bottom right A procession of boats, part of a traditional regatta, glides past the old railway station, completed in 1861, on the site of the demolished church of Santa Lucia. Also visible is the Ponte degli Scalzi (1858), the iron bridge erected during the period of Austrian rule.

42 top Pictures of the First World War: the horses of St. Mark were taken down from the basilica and a place was temporarily found for them, protected by sandbags, inside the Doges' Palace. Later they were transported by barge to the mainland, first to Cremona, then Ostiglia, and finally Rome, where they were installed in the garden of Palazzo Venezia. Once the war was over, they were returned to Venice.

42-43 Measures were taken to protect the exterior of St. Mark's during the First World War.

43 top In 1934 Shakespeare's The Merchant of Venice was performed in Campo di San Trovaso, under the direction of Max Reinhardt, to inaugurate the first Festival del Teatro. With "stage sets" designed by architect Duilio Torres, the boat-building yard at San Trovaso was transformed into a 16th-century loggia.

43 centre right During the Fascist era St. Mark's Square was often used for events organized to support the regime: mass rallies, oath-taking ceremonies for the youth movements, visits by the duce. In June 1934, the meeting between Hitler and Mussolini, the first official step in the pact between Nazi-Socialism and Fascism, took place here.

43 bottom right Venice succumbs to the disastrous floods of November 4, 1966. During the longest day in the history of their city, the Venetians' amazing faith in the ability of their city to survive was cruelly tested: as the lagoon struggled to expel the tide of "acqua alta," Venice and her islands risked sinking forever.

44-45 and 44 top
The Basilica St. Mark
has always been
intimately connected
with the seat of
government. It was
the ducal chapel of the
Palatium, in keeping
with late-Roman and
Byzantine tradition.
From its very earliest
days Venice had close
ties with the Near East
and Byzantium, a fact
that is evident in every
element of this splendid
structure, with its
five domes, modelled
on the church of the
Holy Apostles in
Constantinople. It
was consecrated in
1094. The then doge,
Vitale Falier,
invented an
incredible tale about
the body of St. Mark
being miraculously
found inside one of
the pillars of the
basilica during
construction.

Few cities on earth can boast an artistic heritage to rival that of Venice. Exploring Venice is like visiting a huge floating museum, a showcase of man's creative talents through the ages: from the Byzantine world to Romanesque and flamboyant Gothic; from the splendours of the Renaissance to the exuberance of the Baroque and Rococo; from the noble simplicity of Neo-classicism to the harmony and elegance of Art Nouveau. Venice offers all this in amazing abundance, in its architecture, sculptures, paintings and decorative arts. The Venetians of old were not only merchants. They were men of exceptionally good taste, and a depth of feeling that set them apart from other peoples. No one could stand before the mosaics in St. Mark's and fail to be moved by their message, combining religion with the spirituality of art. The most compelling sacred stories from the Bible are told in pictures, instantly legible even by the illiterate and ignorant. As the poet Diego Valeri wrote in his celebrated *Guida Sentimentale di Venezia (Sentimental Guide to Venice)*, these mosaics are a synthesis of the very beginnings of a stunning creation, the city of Venice: radiating from the "pages" of the mosaics is "that heroic spirit which reconciles faith in Christ and faith in the splendid works of man, and which is the ethical root of the commercial, political and warfaring — as well as artistic — greatness of Venice."

The basilica is an imposing monument, a worthy resting place for the mortal remains of the city's patron saint, Mark the Evangelist.

The first church on this site (which has always been the Doges' Chapel, attached to the palace of government) was consecrated under Doge Giovanni Partecipazio I in 832; it was destroyed by fire in 967 during an uprising of the Venetian people. Rebuilt soon after, it underwent further restructuring from 1060 onwards, until its consecration in 1094, when Vitale Falier was doge. It was still a bare, austere church built of exposed brick, with a central plan in the form of a Greek cross and five domes. The crucial year for its transformation was undoubtedly 1204 when, after the sack of Constantinople, splendid riches — the spoils of war — arrived in Venice. Among these trophies were the four horses in gilded bronze, immediately placed on the loggia of St. Mark's

45 *Venice had a strange love/hate relationship with Byzantium. Historians look upon the choice of St. Mark as patron saint — in the place of St. Theodore, intrinsically linked with the Byzantine brand of Christianity — as the city-state's first real step towards autonomy and independence from the capital of the Empire of the East. The second, much more explicit step was the conquest of Constantinople in 1204, providing spoils used to further embellish the basilica.*

46 *The atrium, or narthex, of St. Mark's originally extended around three sides of the nave. As a result of major structural changes when the Baptistry and Zen Chapel were built, it was eventually closed on the right side, facing Piazzetta San Marco. The mosaics illustrating Old Testament stories are a stunning ornamental feature of this area. These masterpieces were among the basilica's very earliest mosaics and, in terms of colour, technique and finesse, they exemplify the highest pitch of accomplishment of 13th-century Venetian craftsmen.*

47 left In addition to wonderfully ornate mosaics St. Mark's has a beautiful polychrome marble floor. It was created from very rare marble of the finest quality taken from the fabulous Oriental dwellings plundered during the sack of Constantinople.

47 top right The Baptistry, also called the Church of the Putti, came into being when the basilica was restructured in the first half of the 14th century. Its vast area is comprised of three bays with domical vault ceilings; at its centre is the baptismal font, designed by Jacopo Sansovino.

47 bottom right In the dome containing 24 scenes from the Book of Genesis, *the mosaics are divided into three areas, depicting the episodes of "Creation of Heaven and Earth," "Adam and Eve in the Garden of Eden" and "Temptation, Sin and Banishment." Completing the dome's sparkling mosaics are four seraphs in the corner spandrels and "Tales of Cain and Abel" in the lunettes.*

façade, by the central arch. The spoils also included what was subsequently the corpus of the fabulous Treasure of St. Mark: liturgical objects, precious reliquaries and priceless marble statues. In the thirteenth century the domes were raised and covered with sheets of lead resting on a wooden frame. Decorating the interior continued into the fifteenth century by which time the building, with its precious marble and mosaics, had acquired the radiant, shimmering colours that still enchant visitors today.

Supreme testimony to the greatness of

the Venetian people, the basilica has for centuries occupied pride of place in the spacious square that takes its name. It is the only square in Venice to merit the title of *piazza*, a fact that elevates it and differentiates it with respect to the city's other large open spaces, known simply as *campi*.

A short distance away, beside the Doges' Chapel, stands another architectural splendour, the Doges' Palace with its magnificent Scala d'Oro, immense halls, the private apartments of the doge and the huge Sala del Maggior Consiglio (Chamber of the Great Council).

48-49 The most striking feature of the basilica's interior is the dazzling mosaics, which extend the whole length of the church, as effectively shown here, looking down the nave towards the presbytery.

"Letting your eyes and soul roam around the enchanted garden of mosaics — wrote the poet Diego Valeri — you feel a sense of not only magical but thoroughly and supremely human exhaltation."

50-51 The "Pentecost" and "Ascension" domes: in the centre the Holy Spirit, portrayed as a dove, descends on the Apostles with tongues of fire; between the windows, people wait to receive the apostolic message in their own tongue. In the dome on the right of the photo is the Ascension of Christ, a feast close to the hearts of Venetians because of their Ascension Day ceremony of the Wedding to the Sea.

52 top and 52-53 *The Doges' Palace was the seat of government of the Serenissima, glory and figurehead of the power of the dominante. But the Venetians also turned it into a cradle of art. As well as a magnificent residence for the doge, this building was the seat of government and* housed the law-courts and public archives. All the most significant moments in the history of this seafaring republic centred on this building: it witnessed the birth of a great state, ruler of lands and seas, and — after a thousand years of "gala performances" — the swan song that preceded its demise.*

53 top The Porta della Carta, the imposing main doorway named after the nearby archives where all the state's documents were kept, leads into the inner courtyard of the Doges' Palace. The most striking feature here is the Scala dei Giganti (Giants' Staircase), built by Antonio Rizzo between 1484 and 1501 after a fire destroyed the doge's private apartments in 1483. The giants in question are Neptune and Mars, statues by Jacopo Sansovino that, as a mythological reference, clearly symbolize supremacy over land and sea.

Dark secret passageways lead to the Sala del Consiglio dei Dieci (meeting-place of the Council of Ten, established to "protect the subjects of the Republic from the abuses of personal power"): here the accused was confronted with evidence presented by mysterious, unknown informers who had entrusted their circumstantiated indiscretions or simple poisonous lies to the "post-box" mouths of stone lions, always greedy for more. From close at hand the accused heard the sound of creaking locks, engraved with the initials of the dreaded Council. He may have been led to the room of the Council's Inquisitors, the doors of the Torture Chamber swinging open to reveal a sinister-looking rope, an indication of the torment still to come. The atmosphere in these rooms is dense with history and the literature it inspired: George Byron's *Marin Falier*, the black veil painted on the frieze of the Council Chamber, with its forbidding words: "*Hic est locus Marini Falieri decapitati pro criminibus*" (Here is the place of Marin Falier, beheaded for his crimes). Crossing the Bridge of Sighs, the cloak-and-dagger scenarios of Romantic literature acquire a new and vivid meaning, although the image of this place conveyed by colourful historical novels is far more sinister than reality. The cells of the Piombi and Pozzi prisons offer a further opportunity to let the imagination roam, with mental pictures of famous escapes, like the spectacular getaway of Giacomo Casanova, prince of adventurers and libertines: scenes brought to mind by nineteenth-century illustrations by Bayard in Bernard's *Les évasions célèbres illustrées* or by Italian Nerbini Editions. Every art lover can be satiated in Venice, for its broad-spanning heritage offers an almost endless array of masterpieces.

In its privileged position on St. Mark's Square, the Museo Correr contains some of the city's very finest collections. It owes its existence to a Venetian nobleman and prosperous merchant, Teodoro Correr (1750–1830), a keen collector of art and "memorabilia" connected with the history of Venice. The museum's collections have been further enlarged by numerous donations and bequests. Its picture gallery and prestigious collection of relics and curios allow present-day visitors to reconstruct the most significant historic events of the Serenissima: banners, arms, coins, books, paintings of historic scenes, the *corno* cap worn by the doge, as well as many rooms of precious paintings from Veneto and elsewhere (this part of the museum was reopened in 1960, its interiors renovated by Carlo Scarpa). Other periods of history covered by the collections are the Risorgimento and nineteenth-century Venice, a less glorious time for the city, from the fall of the Republic to conquest by the Austrians and French and eventual annexation to the Kingdom of Italy.

During its splendid past, Venice has

54 top The Scala d'Oro (Golden Staircase) starts from the middle of the east loggia. Commenced to the plans of Sansovino but completed by Scarpagnino in 1559, it was given this name on account of the richness of its ornate white and gilt stucco decorations.

54 bottom
The largest room in the Doges' Palace is the Sala del Maggior Consiglio (Great Council Chamber). Here the patricians, assembled to pass laws and to elect the most important officials of their city-state, sat on benches arranged lengthwise, presided over by the doge and signoria. The room was also used on ceremonial occasions and for public festivities. Light streams through its seven ogival and two rectangular windows, illuminating the gilded ceiling. After its destruction by fire in 1577, it was rebuilt by the architect Antonio Da Ponte and completed with Tintoretto's huge Paradise on the rear wall.

also been a preeminent centre of printing and a feast awaits the eyes of book lovers at the Biblioteca Nazionale Marciana: a vast collection of books, incunabula and beautifully illuminated manuscripts, including precious Aldine editions bearing the unmistakable anchor and dolphin emblem. The library owes much of its remarkable collection to the fall of Constantinople to the Turks (1453). Many scholars fled, taking with them rare old manuscripts. In 1468, Cardinal Bessarion — patriarch of Constantinople — expressed his gratitude for the welcome he received in the city considered a second Byzantium by donating to Venice his outstanding library, richly endowed with Greek and Latin codices. The Serenissima commissioned Jacopo Sansovino to design a worthy home for these exceptional collections. The library, which became known as the Libreria Sansoviniana, was the realization of a project conceived by Francesco Petrarca almost a century earlier.

Ancient art also has a prominent place in Venice, with an ad hoc museum: the Museo Archeologico, in Piazzetta San Marco. Most of the original Greek and Roman sculptures exhibited here once belonged to the Grimani family. The museum owes the corpus of its collections — including outstanding Roman coins and jewellery — to Domenico Grimani, cardinal, theologian and humanist, and his nephew Giovanni, patriarch of Aquileia, renowned for his passionate interest in classical civilizations.

To visit the city's most important art museum we must leave St. Mark's Square and make our way — on foot or by water-bus — to the wooden Ponte dell'Accademia.

The prestigious collection of artworks contained in the Gallerie dell'Accademia illustrates the history of Venetian painting from the fourteenth to the eighteenth century. It is housed in a group of buildings of unique monumental and architectural value: the fifteenth-century church of Santa Maria della Carità, with its three apsidal chapels; the monastery of the order of Canonici Lateranensi, with testimonies to the work of Palladio; the Scuola della Carità, famous for its carved wood coffered ceiling with elegant gilt ornamentation.

A series of polyptychs (with figures of the Madonna and saints prominent against a gold background) offers an ideal starting point for a visit to the galleries: they are an emphatic statement of the move away from Byzantine culture towards the innovative style of international Gothic. Next come rooms containing all the finest paintings of Giovanni Bellini, in particular the series of Madonnas, lyrical expressions of spirituality dosed with mysticism. In the sanctum sanctorum is Giorgione's *The Tempest*: this stunning pastoral symphony exudes mystery and sensuality; it is a poem to nature, a landscape in which lightning flashes across the sky, throwing a sinister light on a Veneto town, mirrored in the river on which it stands. This wonderful panorama of Venetian painters includes a late Titian with the sombre colours of his celebrated *Pietà*, huge canvases painted by Tintoretto and Paolo Veronese's *Feast at the House*

55 top The Sala del Senato (Senate Room) — also called "Sala dei Pregadi" was used by a political body formed of 60 patricians elected by the Great Council. Membership was an honour conferred for distinguished service in public office or in administrative or military fields.

55 bottom As the name indicates, the Sala del Collegio is where the Collegio met. One of the most important authorities of the Serenissima, it comprised the doge, six councillors, the "Savi" (the leaders of the Council of Ten), and the Great Chancellor. Built by Antonio da Ponte and based on plans by Palladio and Rusconi, the room has a coffered ceiling, exquisitely carved and gilded.

of Levi. The improprieties and profane atmosphere of this painting — originally intended as a Last Supper — caused Veronese, in 1573, to be brought to trial before the ecclesiastical tribunal of the Inquisition, under suspicion of heresy. The accessory figures in his painting — German soldiers clearly the worse for drink, a buffoon with a parrot, a serving man with a bloody nose — met with definite disapproval. Obliged to justify his action, he denied indecorum and claimed the absolute right of artistic licence to which painters were entitled, as were "poets and madmen." Asked to state exactly who was present at the Supper, Veronese did not hesitate: "I believe Christ and his Apostles were there but if there is space leftover in my painting, I invent decorative figures to fill it." This bold and eloquent self-defence on the part of an artist must surely have brought a glimmer of a smile to the lips of the surly Inquisitors.

All the great names of Venetian painting are present in the Gallerie dell'Accademia. The eighteenth century is represented by its finest painters: Guardi, Canaletto, Marieschi, Bellotto. The pastels of Rosalba Carriera portray powdered society ladies and elegantly attired dandies. The episodes of domestic life painted by Pietro Longhi contain the kind of characters described by Goldoni's lively pen, in pictures resembling scenes from a comic play.

The great cycle of the *Miracles of the True Cross* takes visitors back to the late fifteenth century and painters of ceremonial occasions, like Gentile Bellini and Vittore Carpaccio. Their huge paintings show the procession in St. Mark's Square, or a superb Rialto Bridge, when it was still made of wood. Carpaccio's finest work is undoubtedly *The Legend of Saint Ursula,* a cycle that narrates the eulogistic tale of the legendary and beautiful Ursula, princess of Brittany. It starts when her hand in marriage is asked by Ereo, son of the pagan king of England: after the meeting with Pope Cyriac in front of Castel Sant'Angelo, it tells of the misadventures that befall her, ending with the martyrdom and apotheosis of the saint. Of all the scenes depicted, the *Dream of Ursula* is the most enchanting: in an atmosphere of calm and tranquility, purity and poetry, the virgin Ursula lies asleep on her pristine bed! A magical silence reigns in the room, described in the minutest detail by Carpaccio's brush. Every object is charged with symbolism, but never overcharged. Death and martyrdom may await her but the saintly smile on

58 In 1537–1553 the Senate commissioned Jacopo Sansovino to design a building, in the Piazzetta, to house the legacy of Cardinal Bessarione; it became the core of the future Biblioteca Marciana. Its double stairway with vaulted ceiling and domes above the landings leads up to the library. Most prominent in the Sala Dorata (Gilded Room), so named because of its ceiling, are paintings by Veronese, who was chosen to decorate the room by the Procuratori upon recommendations from Sansovino and Titian.

59 top Along the ground floor of the library, built to the plans of Jacopo Sansovino, are Doric columns with alternating metopes and triglyphs on the entablature; the frieze of the Ionic order in the gallery is decorated with putti and garlands. The building was completed by Vincenzo Scamozzi in 1588, with the last five columns facing the Molo.

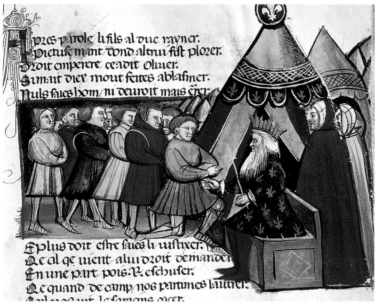

59 centre The Biblioteca Nazionale Marciana is an exceptionally important Venetian institution and a paradise for book lovers, particularly on account of its remarkable collection of illuminated manuscripts.

59 bottom After the fall of the Venetian Republic, the library's collections grew in size with the addition of books and manuscripts from religious communities closed by Napoleon.

In 1904 it moved into the sombre Zecca, the mint where the Serenissima made its coins. Today it occupies its original historic site as well as the mint.

Ursula's innocent face reveals her absolute trust in prayer and in God, her sole joy and redemption.

It is now time to get to know one of the most splendid periods in the history of Venice, the 1700s. What tourist hasn't dreamed of being transported — disguised perhaps with hooded cloak and half-mask — into one of the magnificent *palazzi* of the eighteenth century, perhaps because it was the last in the glorious existence of the Serenissima Republic? Imagination can work wonders in Venice, where even reality is imbued with magic. In the superlative setting offered by Ca' Rezzonico at San Barnaba, the Museo del Settecento Veneziano presents Venice at its most fascinating — and most decadent — by providing an insight into the everyday life of a patrician household. Interior decorations, furniture, accessories, precious lacquerwork with exotic motifs evoked by a world of fantasy: a China similar to the one that existed in the comedies and tales of Carlo Gozzi. The museum provides an ideal setting for the masks of the *Commedia dell'Arte*, amid the acrobat Pulcinellas painted by Giandomenico Tiepolo, brought here from Villa Tiepolo at Zianigo, as well as for exhibits testifying to the splendours of Carnival, secrets of the bed-chamber and idle chatter of the boudoir. The entire *settecento* is present here in lavish style, exemplified by a monumental *bureau trumeau* in finest burled walnut; paintings by Pietro Longhi ("genre" interi-

60 top Gentile
Bellini painted the
Stories of the Cross
for the Scuola di San
Giovanni
Evangelista (School
of St.John the
Evangelist) at the
end of the 1400s. In
the episode seen here,
the artist
demonstrates his
talents as a painter
of portraits as well as
descriptive views. An

amazing number of
figures, including
personages like
Caterina Cornaro,
queen of Cyprus, are
depicted with
meticulous detail;
also visible are the
Fondamenta and
Rio di San Lorenzo,
setting of the Miracle
of the Cross a large
painting by the artist
now in the Gallerie
dell'Accademia.

60-61 The huge
Feast in the House of
Levi by Paolo Caliari,
known as Veronese, is
exhibited in the
Gallerie
dell'Accademia: this
intended Last Supper
caused the artist a
great many problems.
On account of its
profanity and
improprieties, he was
called before the
Inquisition. He got
out of trouble only by
renaming the picture.

ors or Goldoni-style "Carnival pranks"); luminous views by Canaletto and Guardi; chinoiserie and the glittering splendour of Murano chandeliers. Reassembled here is an entire pharmacy, *Ai do San Marchi*, seemingly straight out of Longhi's painting of *The Pharmacist*, with its row of jars marked with names of exotic medicinal herbs: *theriac* — universal cure-all, its ingredients a mystery — occupies a prominent place. Lastly, there is the marionette theatre from Palazzo Grimani, waiting for someone to manipulate the strings and bring the figures to life. The marionettes are close relations of the puppets seen shortly before in a painting in which the audience — behind a grille — is formed of nuns of San Zaccaria: hardly a great consolation for daughters of patrician households forced to take the veil by an insane practice devised to keep families' assets intact, to be inherited entirely by the firstborn son. A tour of the patrician homes scenically situated along the Grand Canal would not be complete without a visit to Ca' d'Oro, an outstanding example of Venetian palace architecture. The building also contains numerous items testifying to the city's multifarious contributions to painting and the decorative arts. In 1984, after extensive restructuring and

61 top left The most
glorious painting to
be seen in the Gallerie
dell'Accademia is
Giorgione's Tempest,
an authentic poem to
nature. Mood is
conveyed by evocative
use of colour, but the
theme also reveals an
unusual and until
then unknown
freedom of expression.

61 top right Francesco
Guardi transports us
to the heart of St.
Mark's Basin, with the
dark colours typical of
his later works, with this view of the island
of San Giorgio
Maggiore (in the
Gallerie
dell'Accademia).
It was a subject he painted several times,
on this occasion —
according to art
historians — with the
collaboration of his
son, Giacomo.

renovation, the Galleria Giorgio Franchetti in Ca' d'Oro was reopened to the public. It contains collections left to the Italian State in 1916 by baron Giorgio Franchetti. No visitor could fail to be impressed by this gem of Venetian Gothic architecture: just beyond the doorway, for instance, is a fifteenth-century wellhead by Bartolomeo Bon, exuberantly embellished with Gothic leaf-work. The collections are interdisciplinary, as Franchetti himself intended, with sculpture, bronzes, medals and paintings of the Flemish school from the depositories of the Gallerie dell'Accademia; also exhibited here are frescoes by Giorgione and Titian, removed from the walls of the Fondaco dei Tedeschi, near the Rialto Bridge. Not long ago the Conton ceramics collection was also installed in Ca' d'Oro, in rooms taken from the adjoining Palazzo Duodo; among the exhibits are pieces of old Venetian ceramics unearthed now and again on the sandbanks of the lagoon.

A short distance from centrally located Campo di Santa Maria Formosa is an attractive patrician palazzo once owned by the Querini Stampalia family; it is now an important private foundation and library, with many old books regarding local culture. When count Giovanni Querini Stampali died in 1868, he had established in his will that his immense fortune be used to finance a foundation and a library: this library was to be kept open as much as possible, and especially when other city libraries were closed. The splendid art gallery makes the visit well worthwhile. Besides some fine works by Pietro Longhi and a rich collection of fourteenth- to eighteenth-century paintings, its attractions include a series of 69 pictures by Gabriel Bella, a minor painter of importance because of the subjects he chose. His scenes of Venetian festivals and leisure-time pursuits include bull chases, bear chases, regattas on the Grand Canal (including a curious 'cart' race), a soccer match, polo fights between the opposing factions of Castellani and Nicolotti, the Labours of Hercules (a contest that involved building human pyramids), colourful carnivals, a frozen lagoon dotted with skaters and endless other views of the city that offer insight into Venice of happier, bygone days. Venice hosts the Biennale, a milestone event in the world of contemporary art, and also has a Galleria d'Arte Moderna, installed in Ca' Pesaro. Regrettably, not all the major works presented at Biennale exhibitions between 1895 and the present day can be seen here, but the gallery has many excellent exhibits, including a significant collection of nineteenth-century Veneto painters (Milesi, Ciardi, Favretto, Nono). Also housed in Palazzo Pesaro, on the third floor, is the Museo d'Arte Orientale, based on the collection of Enrico di Borbone, count of Bardi. His eclectic collection — originally installed in Palazzo Vendramin Calergi (where he lived) — was put together during a

63 bottom In a painting from the cycle of the Miracles of the Holy Cross — the episode of the reliquary in which Francesco Querini, patriarch of Grado, is shown exorcizing a devil thanks to its miraculous powers — Vittore Carpaccio depicts a scene from everyday Venetian life. We see the old Rialto Bridge, then still built of wood, with the bascule walkway in the centre to allow the passage of sailing boats. By the early 16th century the wooden bridge was seriously in need of restoration, but it was decided in 1524 to build it anew, in stone to the plans of Antonio Da Ponte.

64 top A further insight into Venetian life is offered by Francesco Guardi in The Nuns' Parlatory *at San Zaccaria.*

65 top left This fine painting of The Grand Canal Looking From Ca' Balbi Towards Rialto *by Canaletto, done in his early years, was bought by Venice City Council in 1983 and is on display in the galleries of Ca' Rezzonico. It is one of the few works by Canaletto still held in a public collection in Venice.*

64 centre Numerous frescoes by Giandomenico Tiepolo were removed from the walls of Villa Zianigo at Mirano in 1906 and installed here in the museum of Ca' Rezzonico. Among them is the famous oval ceiling painting of The Clown's Swing, *a capriccio portraying a carnival-like scene of the kind Venice offered in abundance.*

64-65 and 65 top right Further intriguing scenes from Venetian life are depicted in these two canvases, in the Querini Stampalia museum: Football game at Sant'Alvise *by Gabriel Bella, celebrated chronicler of Venetian festivities, and* Fighting at San Barnaba *by an anonymous 17th-century artist.*

long journey in the Far East. From China there is porcelain, jade and lacquerwork; from Indonesia, weapons and a shadow marionette theatre; from Japan, a vast assortment of arms and armour from the days of the samurai. Present-day Venice continues to have links with the Far East. Its influence can still be seen, for example, in the production of precious damasks made from finest quality materials — silk, cotton, linen, silver and gold thread — inspired by ancient motifs but often with a stylistic content that reveals the talents of contemporary designers. Both Oriental and Ottoman worlds were a source of inspiration to the skilled craftsmen who discovered the secrets of making marbled paper, a technique now also applied to silk, wood and plaster. Venice acquired fame worldwide not only as a great trading power but also as a vibrant centre of arts and crafts. The workmanship of its craftsmen and artisans can be seen in several city museums, for instance Palazzo Mocenigo at San Stae, which houses a museum of textiles and costumes. Displayed in the rooms of this former patrician residence are sacred vestments and samples of fabrics produced on Venetian looms, as well as textiles from Tuscany, Lyons and Flanders, tapestries, eighteenth-century fashion sketches, and costumes from various city collections: a fitting testimony to Venice's still-thriving textile industry.

The Museo Fortuny also has close con-nections with textiles and their production since it is the former home of Mariano Fortuny y Mandrazo, an eclectic figure who was a friend of D'Annunzio, Duse and Diaghilev. His enormous stage- and costume-design workshop was situated in this building (and the costumes he created for the first great female stars of theatre and dance, from Sarah Bernhardt to Eleonora Duse, won him world acclaim). As seen from the exquisite figured and printed fabrics displayed in this museum, Venice has played an important role in the art of textile design and production, with Fortuny a prominent figure in this field. An extraordinary man of many talents (also evident from his photographic archives), he considered Venice the ideal place to live and work.

This panorama of the museums of Venice would not be complete without a mention of the Museo di Ca' del Duca Mocenigo-Le Gallais, a small museum with a lot of charm. The very first coffee houses (*bottega del caffè*) opened in Venice and the tradition fortunately still lives on. So it seems highly appropriate that the city have a museum dedicated to the coffee cult, with a collection that includes hundreds of pieces of bone china: cups as light as a feather, in a multitude of decorative styles and colours. Visitors are transported — in spirit — to the nearby, tiny rooms at Florian's, Quadri's, Lavena's, the glorious cafés of Venetian tradition. Here they join the last

66-67 *This photo of Palazzo Grassi was taken during the 1988 exhibition on the Phoenicians. A major renovation and refurbishment scheme by architects Gae Aulenti and Antonio Foscari has not only restored this palace to its former splendour; it has also provided Venice with an exhibition venue of international standing.*

Venetians, who sit savouring the international climate of Piazza San Marco, the "loveliest drawing-room in the world." And as people come and go, stopping to enjoy a cup of coffee and pass the time of day with familiar faces or total strangers, the scene is neatly summed up in the words of a vernacular poet:

Delightful café with its hoard of memories, where every nation convivially gathers, where the atmosphere is always cheerful and even the silliest person can pass for wise; in your pleasant rooms people learn the real meaning of "dolce far niente,".... and to pass their day in a carefree way, they make every effort to do just nothing.
(Attilio Sarfatti, *Rime veneziane*)

66 top left
Longhena's Ca' Pesaro is a masterpiece of Baroque architecture, centred on the contrast between its vibrant rusticated basements and vast areas of shade created by the building's large windows. This important patrician palazzo now hosts two museums for the city's modern art and Oriental art collections.

66 top right
Palazzo Grassi was designed by Giorgio Massari, considered Baldassare Longhena's heir, and its elegant but severe façade is a foretaste of later neo-classical trends. Construction was started in 1749 and completed in 1766, and the building is one of the finest examples of a patrician residence built not long before the fall of the Republic.

67 top Mariano Fortuny y Mandrazo (1871–1949) — a Spanish painter, sculptor, collector and photographer and an artistic figure of great versatility — made Venice his permanent home. In 1956 his widow donated the palace where he had lived and worked to the city, to be used for artistic and cultural initiatives. With its displays of printed fabrics, paintings, photographs and scenery designs it offers an eye-opening view of both the artistic world of the early 1900s and Fortuny's amazing and multifaceted talents.

67 right The Venice Biennale has been a point of reference for international art from 1895 right up to the present day. Displayed in the large rooms of Ca' Pesaro — in addition to pictures exemplifying seminal phases in the development of 19th-century painting in Venice — are masterpieces from past Biennale. One of the finest is Gustav Klimt's Judith, here assigned place of honour as the ultimate artistic expression of this artist.

"With the aid of divine Providence, the city of the Venetians has been founded on water, it is encompassed by water, it is defended by water instead of walls: whosoever dares bring harm to the public waters shall therefore be pronounced an enemy of the city and shall be attributed no lesser punishment than one who violates the sacred walls of his native city. This edict shall be valid in perpetuity" (1). So states the Latin inscription, by the humanist Egnatius (Gian Battista Cipelli), on a stone formerly to be seen in the Doges' Palace, seat of the *Magistrato dei Savi alle acque*, established by the Council of Ten in 1501 to oversee the protection and conservation of the precious lagoon environment.

Sadly, the present-day approach to this issue does not reflect the uncompromising and foresighted policies of the past. The man-made city of Venice is now faced with problems caused by its natural environment. But its biggest problems are ones man has caused and continues to cause himself, under cover of a putative improvement in the quality of life. Industrial civilization is the main culprit. And the pollution it causes is made even worse by the runoff from

68 bottom Children playing with the pigeons in St. Mark's Square. Jean Cocteau described Venice as a strange and magical city where pigeons walk and lions fly.

68-69 This aerial view offers further evidence of the scenic splendour of St. Mark's Square.

69 top An aerial view
of the Clock Tower,
with the Moors striking
the hour. Probably
designed by Mauro
Codussi circa 1496, it
has a clock with a dial
decorated with gilt
and enamel; as well
as telling the time,
it shows the phases
of the moon and the
movement of the sun
in the zodiac.

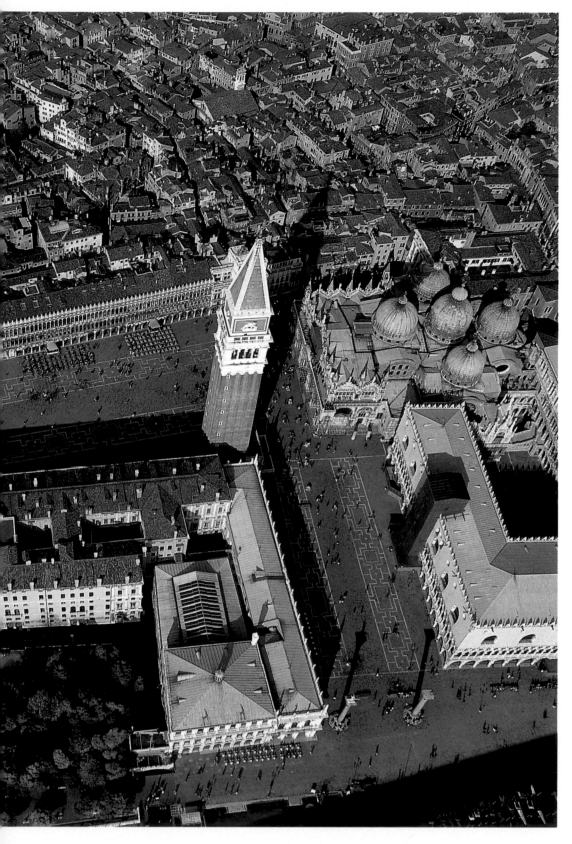

69 bottom
Floods are an
unwelcome but not
infrequent visitor to
Venice, especially in
the area around St.
Mark's Square. For
tourists this is almost
an attraction,
whereas for the people
of Venice it is an ever-
present threat. No one
has forgotten the
tragic floods of
November 1966,
when the water
reached a record
height of over six feet.

70 The Piazzetta and Molo. Visible in the background, high up on one of two towering Oriental granite columns, is the Lion of St. Mark, which was taken to Paris in 1797 and returned in 1815. The statue's unknown origin has led to an incredible amount of conjecture among scholars.

cities and agricultural plants that empty sewage, mineral oils, detergents and residue from fertilizers rich in nitrates and phosphates into the lagoon. The overall outcome is a disturbing deterioration of the lagoon ecosystem: abnormal growth of algae, eutrophication, fish dying in great quantities and total disappearance of the most delicate species, gradual transformation of the lagoon into an enormous swamp, with proliferation of tiresome flies.

The relationship between man and the lagoon environment has totally changed. In order to maintain this extraordinary ecosystem, Venetians of past centuries deviated the course of no fewer than five rivers that once flowed into the lagoon and would eventually have caused its demise. Modern man has instead followed the dictates of indiscriminate industrial development: where once there were only sandbanks, canals and fish hatcheries, new canals have been dug to give access to ports. A new industrial city has been created. If the ongoing battle between the forces of innovation and conservation does not lead to a more responsible approach to this very fragile ecosystem, the future of this age-old city will be sealed with a doleful requiem. There is a lot of truth in an argument constantly repeated by Indro Montanelli, an

authoritative journalist known for his outspoken and often hard-hitting observations. He has always maintained that "a city can be saved only if its citizens want to save it and the Venetians who wanted to save Venice [after the disastrous flood of 1966] were no more than a handful: the others could not see beyond their own everyday lives and their own petty interests."(2) There's no denying that economic interests count for a lot in Venice, and that tourism, with all that it implies, takes centre stage. In the early years of this century tourism's impact was already clearly understood and decried by Filippo Tommaso Marinetti, a leading exponent of the Futurist movement. Somewhat surprisingly, however, his outburst was fired not by his love of Venice but by a desire to put an end to "traditionalist" Venice, saturated with romanticism. Yet even this man who hoped to see the birth of an "industrial and military" city, was not totally immune to its charms: "Enough! enough!...Stop whispering your obscene proposals to everyone who comes your way, Venice, you incorrigible old madam. Beneath your mosaic-embellished attire, you continue to offer debilitating nights of romance, grating serenades and

71 The elegant Renaissance architecture and multicoloured marble of Ca' Dario make it one of the most distinctive palazzi along the Grand Canal. But its fame stems instead from a sinister curse that appears to weigh on all its owners, many of whom have met with violent deaths.

72 top right Ca' Rezzonico, seen here from Palazzo Grassi, was started by Baldassare Longhena and completed in 1750 by Giorgio Massari. Today it hosts the Museo del Settecento Veneziano, offering tourists a chance to relive the carefree atmosphere that pervaded Venice before the demise of the Serenissima.

72 bottom right This magnificent room is in Palazzo Corner Spinelli, once owned by Giovanni Corner, grandson of the queen of Cyprus, Caterina; the building was later acquired by the Spinelli family, highly successful merchants whose wealth came from trading soybeans.

73 Ca' D'Oro (House of Gold) is the gem of Venetian Gothic architecture. Its name is attributable to the gilt finish — no longer visible — that once covered the walls. The building, now home to the Giorgio Franchetti Gallery, was the work of the Lombard stone-carver Matteo Raverti and Venetians Giovanni and Bartolomeo Bon.

*72 left
The imposing Renaissance structure of Ca' Vendramin Calergi is a prominent feature of this stretch of the Grand Canal. The Loredan family commissioned architect Mauro Codussi to design the building in 1481. The composer Richard Wagner lived for a long time on the mezzanine level of the left wing and died here on February 13, 1883. The palace is now the winter quarters of the Municipal Casino.*

cunning ambushes! I too, Venice, once loved the splendid half-darkness of your Grand Canal, with its rare forbidden fruits, and the feverish pallour of your beauties, who descend from balconies on staircases enlaced with moonbeams, flashes of lightning and rivulets of rain, while clashing swords ring out...But you Venetians fix your gormless gaze on your prehistoric lagoons, content to rot in your filthy water, so as to keep filling the coffers of the Company of Grand Hotels, which so carefully prepares for the elegant nights of the rich and famous! What an honour indeed, to play Cupid to their passions." (3)

Fortunately, good sense prevailed. The destructive, avant-garde ideas of Futurism died and Venice remains, having lost none of her seductive charms and ageless beauty. On arriving in Venice (and leaving the ugly Santa Lucia railway station behind), board one of the city's amusing little water-buses: you are instantly aware that you have left what passes for civilization and are entering not a dream but a different, thrilling version of reality.

Outstretched before you is the Grand Canal. "*C'est la plus belle rue que je croy qui soit en tout le monde....*" said Philippe de Commynes, on arriving

74-75 A view of the Grand Canal taken from the point where it is crossed by the San Tomà ferry service. In Venice there are two ways of getting from one side of the Grand Canal to the other: if you're not in a hurry you can catch a vaporetto, *the public water-bus service; alternatively, for a very reasonable charge, you can be gently ferried across the water by two gondoliers in a motorized gondola.*

in Venice as the ambassador of Charles VIII (1494–95). The reaction of today's visitor is no different: overwhelmed by the palaces on either side of the canal, their gaze flits back and forth, for fear of missing some monumental site along this blue, back-to-front "S" that slowly unravels before their eyes. Admittedly, the façades of these buildings have lost some of their splendour: the ornate frescoes that once cast multicoloured reflections on the water are now practically gone; remaining traces continue to fade with the passing years; widening cracks in plaster reveal the relentless march of time. But this, too, is part of the magic of Venice. As Lord Ruskin so convincingly related, every single stone has a story to tell.

The unhurried progress of the waterbus takes the visitor back to a dimension of time previously unknown. Venice needs time; the city was built by time and an element of time is mysteriously locked into its walls and canals. Along the Grand Canal the imposing profile of the eighteenth-century Palazzo Labia, with its huge blocks of Istrian stone, immediately catches your eye. So does — close by — Palazzo Vendramin Calergi, last home of the composer Richard Wagner. A short way further on, on the opposite side, is the

78-79 Palazzo
Giustinian is where
Richard Wagner
composed Act II of
Tristan and Isolde.

This fine Gothic
structure, dating
back to the second
half of the 15th
century, stands next

to another splendid
Gothic building, Ca'
Foscari; the
University of Venice
now occupies its
spacious rooms.

78 top The 12th- to
13th-cenury fondaco
(merchant's home-
cum-warehouse)
handed over to the
Turkish community
by Doge Antonio
Priuli in 1621,
became known as the
Fondaco dei Turchi.
Thorough restoration
in 1858–69 by
Federico Berchet gave
a total facelift to the
façade, with new
arches, two towers
and crenellation,
and disturbed the
beauty of this former
Oriental emporium.

Subsequently bought
by the City Council,
it now houses the
Natural History
Museum.

78 bottom
Overlooking this
picturesque corner of
the Grand Canal are
the early 15th-century
Gothic Palazzo
Pisani-Moretta and
the Palazzo Barbarigo
della Terrazza, so
named on account of
the first-floor terrace
that replaces the part
of the building left
unfinished.

79 top
*The exceptionally
wealthy Labia
family, of Spanish
origin, commissioned
this splendid palace
at San Geremia as
their residence; they
were particularly
proud of it.*

*79 bottom The
spacious main room
of the Gothic Palazzo
Pisani-Moretta
provides an ideal
venue for concerts
and masked balls,
especially at
Carnival time.*

Fondego dei Turchi, with its intriguing battlements: once the property of the Turkish community, this former warehouse-cum-dwelling underwent brutal restoration in the nineteenth century, and an improbable Moorish style was imposed on its double row of arches. Beyond the church of San Stae is the baroque Palazzo dei Pesaro, which now houses the Galleria d'Arte Moderna. Only a matter of yards away is Ca' Corner della Regina, another building that rises resplendent from a rusticated base. The building previously occupying this site was the Venetian residence of Caterina Cornaro, queen of Cyprus; upon the death of James of Lusignan she returned to Venice, where she was welcomed with the title of "daughter of the Republic," and Cyprus — the island set in the sea where Aphrodite was born — came under Venetian dominion.

Ca' d'Oro, with its delightfully "embroidered" arches, is possibly the most celebrated of the city's patrician residences, an authentic gem of Venetian Gothic architecture. Another bend in the canal and you experience the excitement of passing beneath the Rialto Bridge, with its little shops and colourful crowds of tourists. Here, in the heart of Venice, the Grand Canal

80-81 The pleasant vista from the gallery along the façade of St. Mark's — where the four bronze horses look set to gallop off over the city — takes in the Clock Tower and the Square, with its celebrated traditional cafés: Florian's, Lavena's and Quadri's. In the warming rays of the early morning sun tourists crowd their tables, comfortably drinking in the melodious notes of the resident musicians or the first gentle strokes of the bells of the Campanile.

is fronted by a series of palaces bearing the names of great doges: Dandolo, Loredan, Grimani. Here, too, is Palazzo Mocenigo, made famous by the passionate love affairs and idiosyncracies of an eccentric guest, Lord Byron. Tales are told of how he would swim back to his residence in the early hours of the morning, enraged by the lateness of Tita, his trusted gondolier, and go dripping wet through the rooms of Palazzo Mocenigo while his manservant, all too well accustomed to his master's bizarre behavior, came hurrying towards him with dry clothes.

Before reaching the wide bend at Ca' Foscari, Palazzo Barbarigo della Terrazza comes into view, then Palazzo Pisani Moretta with its splendid six-sided windows. The sight of this building led Goethe to talk of a famous painting by Paolo Veronese and to comment on the diversity of two cultures: "The eye is clearly educated by the objects it gets used to seeing, from infancy; this is why the Venetian painter inevitably sees everything as more luminous and more serene than others. We people of the north spend our lives in a monotonous land, made ugly by mud and dust, a place where every beam of light is dulled. We live in confined spaces and, in our countries, cannot imagine such an uplifting spectacle." (4) It was at Ca' Foscari that the great doge Francesco died, after 34 long years of loyal service to the Serenissima.

He was forced to retire from office and the last days of his life were spent painfully witnessing the tribulations of his only son, Jacopo, brought to trial on several occasions and eventually obliged to end his days far from Venice.

By the sharp bend in the Grand Canal stand two more imposing buildings: Palazzo Grassi, built by Giorgio Massari, and — practically opposite on the other side — Palazzo Rezzonico, a baroque patrician residence started by Longhena and completed by Massari. Carlo Rezzonico lived here before he became pope, taking the name Clemente XIII, and a commemorative stone recalls that Robert Browning stayed and died in this building: "Open my heart and you will see engraved inside of it Italy."

The elegant wooden structure of the eternally temporary Ponte dell'Accademia comes into view. This is the last stretch of the Grand Canal and the distinctive domed profile of S.Maria della Salute can be seen in the distance, towering over the surrounding buildings. But the canal still has many splendours to reveal: *Casetta Rossa*, where D'Annunzio wrote his *Notturno*; on the opposite bank, the unfinished façade of Palazzo Venier dei Leoni, where the American Peggy Guggenheim took up residence when she arrived in Venice in 1949 and later installed her splendid collection of contemporary art. Not to be missed further along is Ca' Dario, now slightly

82-83 No tourist can leave Venice without paying a visit to the celebrated cafés in St. Mark's Square. Florian's, the oldest of these historic hangouts, dates back to 1720, when it was opened by the then unknown Floriano Francesconi, who little suspected his modest business would eventually become one of the world's most illustrious cafés.

84-85 It rarely snows in Venice in winter so the occasional snowfall becomes a special event, even reported in the national press and shown on TV news programmes. Waking up to see the city blanketed in snow is certainly a unique experience, as these pictures testify: the first is a view from the Campanile, with the Piazza and Punta della Dogana coated in pristine whiteness; the second shows the old squero at San Trovaso; next come Campo di Santo Stefano, Fondamenta delle Zattere and, lastly, the Clock Tower with the Moors.

tilted, famous for its multicoloured marble walls and — no less — for its sense of dark foreboding, since a strange curse seems still to weigh upon all its owners. As the canal comes to its end — in this last stretch where the ghosts of Venice still linger — it widens to form the splendid St. Mark's Basin. The finest way to experience the almost undescribable thrill of one's first breathtaking sight of Venice is undoubtedly to arrive in the lagoon by boat, even in no grander style than on the ferry that connects Punta Sabbioni with St. Mark's Square. The first impression made by the city could not be expressed more effectively than by Thomas Mann, in the words of his alter ego Gustav von Aschenbach: "He saw it once more, that landing-place that takes the breath away, that amazing group of incredible structures the Republic set up to meet the awe-struck eye of the approaching seafarer: the airy splendour of the palace and Bridge of Sighs, the columns of lion and saint on the shore, the glory of the projecting flank of the fairy temple, the vista of gateway and clock. Looking, he thought that to come to Venice by the station is like entering a palace by the back door. No one should approach, save by the high seas as he was doing now, this most improbable of cities."(Thomas Mann, *Death in*

86-87 Another magical picture of Venice as snow creates an unusual contrast with the black of gondolas moored at the Orseolo Basin landing area, a short way from St. Mark's Square.

85

Venice, translation by H.T. Lowe-Porter, 1928), Venice deserves much more than fleeting visits to the highlights of traditional tourist itineraries. An ideal place to start a more in-depth tour of the city on foot is the essentially proletarian *sestiere* of Castello. From San Zaccaria make your way towards the church of San Giorgio dei Greci, with its bell tower. When exploring the narrow streets of Venice it is wise to follow your instinct rather than your map. Getting lost in this labyrinth increases the excitement and you may despair of ever finding your way out of its winding alleys. On the other side of the short quayside, cosmopolitan Venice, melting pot of peoples and races, presents one of its many faces: the Byzantine features of the Greek-Orthodox community, exemplified in the wonderful icons conserved in the Museum of the Istituto Ellenico.

Your journey continues in search of yet another civilization. From Salizada dei Greci it is only a few yards to the Scuola Dalmata dei Santi Giorgio e Trifone, — also called San Giorgio degli Schiavoni. Its interior houses splendid paintings by Carpaccio, whose narrative talents are revealed in a mélange of reality and fantasy, epic stories and personal experiences, Venetian and far-distant cultures. A few steps on and

88-89 A partial view of the Grand Canal with the Church of the Salute. On a winter's day a leaden overcast sky, the sombre olive green waters of the lagoon and the pristine white of snow on rooftops give a totally new look to the city.

90 At night, dimly
lit by the pale beams
of street lamps, Venice
dons her most
romantic garb. A
cloak of darkness
descends over the still
grey waters of the

lagoon. The ghostly
silence is broken only
by the mesmerizing
sound of gently
splashing water,
eliciting sudden
memories of great
passions of the past.

91-92-93-94 As the
sun goes down, the
Punta della Dogana
and the Church of the
Salute are bathed in
fiery red light. In
1630 a terrible
plague swept through
Venice, decimating
the population. Once
its effects had waned,
the government

decided to erect this
church as a thanks-
offering for
deliverance. Standing
on one of the finest
sites in the city,
overlooking St. Mark's
Basin, this imposing
octagonal structure
was designed by the
architect Baldassare
Longhena.

95 The water-bus
landing area Rialto,
on a foggy night.
Fog is no stranger
to Venice.
The Venetians call it,
almost fondly, caligo.
Thick mists often
sweep swiftly —
in the space of seconds

— and silently
across the city,
submerging it in a
uniform silvery
blanket that blots out
all colour. People
wisely watch their
step: Venice
can be treacherous as
well as charming.

96 bottom left
Tourists exploring the narrow streets around Campo Manin, right in the heart of Venice, may turn down Calle della Vida and come face to face with Palazzo Contarini, a pearl of Venetian

architecture. The building is now commonly known as Palazzo Contarini del Bovolo, after its magnificent external spiral staircase (in Venetian dialect the word "bovolo" means snail).

96 top left
High water causes serious problems in the Rialto area: at the foot of the bridge is the city's biggest fruit and vegetable market, where tourists as well as Venetians come to shop.

you come to the former hospital of St. Caterina and the church of San Giovanni dei Cavalieri di Malta; in this setting, tales of Knights Templars, Knights of St. John of Jerusalem, Rhodes, Malta, and many more are brought back to memory.

The Arsenal, with its imposing walls, is the next prominent site. It has stood on this spot since 1104 when, according to tradition, Doge Ordelaffo Falier ordered its construction; occupying an area of 79 acres (the entire city of Venice covers 1,655 acres), it has witnessed nine centuries of history during which Venice developed, expanded and eventually declined as a great sea power. Situated beyond the centre but midway between the seats of the republic's political authority and its spiritual leader (first bishop, then patriarch), it is the supreme example of an entirely state-controlled industrial and military enterprise. Venice would be unthinkable without its Arsenal, for only thanks to its amazing production capacity was the Serenissima able to hold off the attacks of its many enemies, from pirates to Turks. Even the fertile imagination of Dante Alighieri was fired by this hive of frenzied activity, a hell-on-earth where people worked in terrible conditions for the glory of the

96 right Traffic is always plentiful in the rii, *the smaller canals that criss-cross the water-filled maze of this already complicated city. All kinds of barges and boats unload goods to be delivered to the numerous shops: often their delivery round includes* bacari, *old Venetian taverns not*

to be missed by connoisseurs of good wine and foodies in search of local gastronomic delights. Transportation is no small problem here, since having to carry goods over both water and land sends costs rocketing in Venice. The city is, almost inevitably, the most expensive in Italy.

97 In the narrow streets of Venice physical contact is unavoidable. Nobody ever feels alone here: as soon as you step onto the street, you are confronted and engulfed by every imaginable manifestation of civilized society.

98-99 *Street markets can be found in various parts of Venice, but the most important one is undoubtedly the Rialto market: here, besides stalls selling fruit and vegetables, there is the city's very fine fish market. Strange "floating shops" like those shown in this photo can be seen at the end of Via Garibaldi in the sestiere of Castello (this street was "reclaimed" from a canal, filled in during the Napoleonic era) and in Rio di San Barnaba, close to the Bridge of Fists (Ponte dei Pugni).*

Serenissima. He could have found no more effective way of describing, in his *Inferno*, the infested air that filled the circle of the Evil-Pouches, where immersion in boiling tar was the punishment doled out to corrupt officials, guilty of swindling, fraud and embezzlement of public money: "As in the Arsenal of the Venetians boils in the winter the tenacious pitch to smear their unsound vessels o'er again, for sail they cannot; and instead thereof one makes his vessel new, and one recaulks the ribs of that which many a voyage has made; one hammers at the prow, one at the stern, this one makes oars, and that one cordage twists, another mends the mainsail and the mizzen; thus, not by fire, but by the art divine, was boiling down below there a dense pitch which upon every side the bank belimed." (Dante, *Inferno Canto XXI*, translation by Henry Longfellow, 1867). While making your way along the outer walls of the Arsenal, pause a moment to look at the sundial, marking the slow passage of time. At the end of the quay, turn into Campo della Tana (one meaning of the word "*tana*" is den). The street name derives instead from a dialectal corruption: Venetians once used this name for a place on the banks of the Tanai River, now Don, where they went to procure the hemp needed to make ropes for their ships. At the far end of the Corderie (or rope factory) is an iron bridge, built in the era of Austrian rule. On its other side is a narrow street lined with terraces of late-fifteenth-century buildings: it is a picturesque scene, brought to life by a clutch of old women — nearing the end of long lives spent in this city — who sit busily chatting beneath a multi-coloured "ceiling" of clothes hung to dry. Such sights are increasingly rare, reminders of bygone days when the city was populated by more "real people" and fewer tourists. Consumer society has now wiped out all of this; the irresistible appeal of television traps people in their homes like prisoners. In moments of nostalgia, they can only gaze at elegant old black-and-white photos or seek out these few remaining cameos of the past.

Via Garibaldi is wide and spacious, a fact that immediately strikes the visitor as inconsistent, out of line. Its paving, too, is different. On closer examination you realize that beneath its blocks of red porphyry flow the waters of a small canal. You are walking on water — no less — while surrounded by ordinary elements of everyday life: shops, cafés, taverns, a small market with fish, fruit and vegetable stalls, even a small sailboat, now doubling as a water-borne sales outlet... a corner of Venice untouched by the passage of time.

Your route now takes you towards the island of San Pietro di Castello (known in olden days as Olivolo).

100 Rialto, the old insula realtina *was one of the first areas to be settled, and its market has always been the real heart of Venice and the Grand Canal. All the city's most important trade activities were focused here, with wholesale and retail markets and countless workshops. Sales of spices, fabric, gold* and finely decorated hides centred on this district, as is still evident from the street names, although most of these craft activities have now disappeared from the scene. All that remains are the big fruit and vegetable market and the fish market, reckoned to be the best in the whole Veneto region.

Extending beyond the church, with its separate, leaning campanile in off-white Istrian stone, are meadows, boat-building yards, fishing boats with baskets in which the day's catch is kept, a long iron bridge. It is a still, solemn scene but one that fires the imagination: for docked here at one time were the boats that carried the patriarch from this island, where he resided, to join the Procession of the Bucentaur. And at San Nicolò del Lido, facing you across the lagoon, the gilded vessel carrying the doge in full ceremonial dress awaited the blessing of the ring for the Marriage to the Sea. Yet another face of Venice....

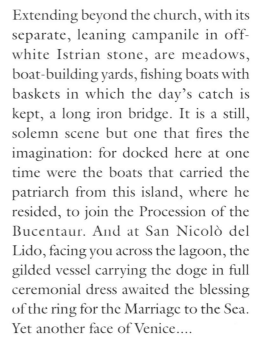

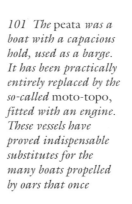

101 The peata *was a boat with a capacious hold, used as a barge. It has been practically entirely replaced by the so-called* moto-topo, *fitted with an engine. These vessels have proved indispensable substitutes for the many boats propelled by oars that once transported goods to every part of the city. The* moto-topo *still retains something of tradition: painted on its sides are colourful friezes and picturesque old names, boldly executed in traditional style and in the best of taste.*

CARNIVAL AND TRADITIONAL VENETIAN FESTIVITIES

102 top left When a group of artists — most of them former students of the local Academy of Fine Arts — opened Venice's first mask shop in 1978, they had no idea their venture would be such an enormous success.

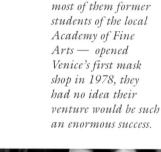

The once packed calendar of traditional festivities celebrated with such gusto in Venice has been notably slimmed down since the late 18th century. No longer are visitors presented with the multifarious array of events that once enhanced the fun-loving reputation of the Serenissima. The rest of Europe saw Venice as a city dedicated to the pursuit of pleasure, with seemingly year-round bacchanalian revelry. To quote from a French guidebook written by Jules Lecompte, very much in vogue in the 19th century: "The round of Venetian festivities echoes across Europe, which once followed her every deed. These wonderful celebrations draw hedonists from all over the continent, pleasure lovers determined to obtain their full share of the caresses of this amazon turned licentious reveler, and to be party to the intrigue of her houses of retreat and the mysteries of her discreet gondolas." The reader pictured scenes of passion and intrigue, the lure of sensual delights amid a maze of *calli* in pursuit of an imaginary female masked figure wearing *tabarro e bautta* (heavy cloak and silk mantle). In his mind's eye he followed her to the Ridotto or another gambling house, ready to exchange some trifling pledge of love, then on to a café or into a gondola,

where the cabin hid the lovers from prying eyes. The ghostlike figures evoked by Lecompte's description really did look like ghosts. Each one wore a *bautta*, a silk mantle with a hood to frame the face and delicate lace around the shoulders; completing the outfit was a three-cornered hat and the distinctive white mask, known to Venetians as the *larva* (Latin word for ghost) or *volto* (face). The last wigged figures of the 1700s were, in effect, little more than ghosts: like many others they refused to see the sad fate that awaited their city, drowning their sorrows in a sea of uninhibited self-indulgence and dissipation. Venice Carnival as we know it today dates back to 1980, and it owes its revival to totally different causes. In earlier centuries this period of festivities was an "institutionally approved" part of the republic's life: it was a time when freedom and transgression were allowed and even encouraged, within a fixed timescale, to divert attention from possible social ills. In costume and mask, once a year, the city's underclass were less aware of their poverty, their disguises serving to eliminate all inequalities. In the corrupt, libertine social scenario of the last years of the Serenissima, a mask served as essential moral cover. Adultery reigned supreme; the excesses of gambling brought entire

102 bottom left Before the revival of Venice Carnival these craftsmen specialized in gilding furniture and frames. To meet demand from a burgeoning new market, they gradually devoted more and more of their time and workshop space to making papier-mâché masks. Certainly a more profitable line of business than a trade that has fewer and fewer customers, in a city with an aging and shrinking population.

102 top right and 103 In present-day Venice masquerading in costume has become an annual ritual once again, although an increasing number of Venetians prefer to refrain: at Carnival time their city is inundated with tourists desperate to show off their finery for the benefit of a willing photographer. To this purpose many of them linger hopefully in fanciful — but tiring — poses in front of the city's most celebrated sights.

104-105 In the 18th century the Venetians loved to take advantage of the anonymity afforded by masks and costumes and to indulge in the licentious atmosphere that prevailed during Carnival. Hordes of pleasure-seeking visitors still pour into Venice at Carnival time, although little of the traditional spirit remains. The "new" Carnival was resuscitated as recently as 1980 to give a boost to the slowest months for tourism. And the response among tourists — unable to resist the combined appeal of Venice and Carnival — has exceeded all expectations, with numbers increasing year by year.

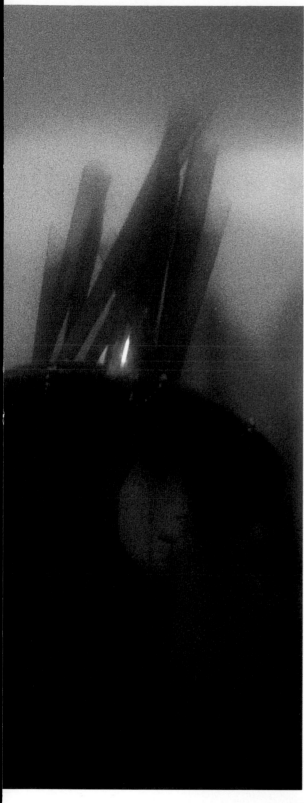

patrician families to their knees and forced nobles to beg on street corners. Masks covered every kind of shame. Society ladies were even required by law to wear a mask, to stop them from parading in splendid jewellery (banned by laws intended to curb extravagance) and to save their husbands from being held up to general ridicule as their marital trials and tribulations were made into public spectacles. Carnival returned to Venice after an absence of almost two hundred years, at the instigation of the Biennale and of the Compagnia dei Grandi Alberghi (CIGA hotel group). The objective of the city's leading cultural institution had been to relaunch Venice as a capital of theatre but this worthy proposal eventually got pushed into the background. The motives of the hotel group were more material: it aimed to give tourism a much-needed boost during the slowest period of the year. But above and beyond these considerations, the underlying philosophy of carnival had changed. Venetians of old wore a disguise in order to conceal their identity; today, in a society where image is everything, carnival costumes and masks are worn to attract notice, to be part of a grand — though short-lived — splurge of pageantry and panache in which each one of us can indulge our desire for self-glorification. A mask used to be worn to lose identity, and to be caught up in a regenerating round of carnival revelry, sensual delights that make the black side of life temporarily fade from view. Today masks no longer serve as a protective shield; on the contrary, in the midst of an anonymous crowd, a masked figure flaunts himself and his finery, hoping perhaps to be immortalized by the lens of some big-name photographer. Masks have also eroded the market share of the once traditional, kitsch souvenir of Venice, the gondola musical box. The number of craftsmen whose work now focuses on making carnival masks has rocketed in recent years. The guild of artisan *mascareri* — specialized makers of papier-mâché and leather masks — has statutes dating back as far as 1436. But for lack of customers the trade eventually died out, to be revived only in 1979 when a group of young artists decided to start a workshop catering to a vast public rather than a theatrical elite. In the wake of the enormous success of Venice's newly instituted carnival has come a big upswing in business. A clear distinction has to be made, however, between real craftsmen and improvised mask-makers, cashing in on the new-found popularity of the Venetian carnival. And the same applies — as we shall see — to the art of glassmaking. But rather than

quibble over the merits of decorative arts and crafts in present-day Venice, let us return to the city's festivities. The Feast of the Ascension, called *La Sensa* in Venetian dialect, is one of the most important, also on account of its historic and sacramental significance, embodied in the symbolic ritual of the Marriage to the Sea. Admittedly this ancient ceremony has lost much of its sanctimonious solemnity. Since the splendid gilded Bucentaur no longer exists, participants and onlookers now have to make do with an elegant *bissona* (an eight-oar gala gondola). The doge used to be carried across the lagoon in the Bucentaur — followed by a colourful procession of gondolas — to cast into the sea the ring that symbolically reasserted the supremacy of Venice over the Adriatic. For centuries the ceremony had an overwhelming aura of solemnity and pageantry, although foreigners among the spectators occasionally indulged in malicious comments of the sort mockingly penned by Joachim Du Bellay, in his *Regrets* (1558): "What a splendid sight, Magny, these magnificent buffoons, with their wonderful Arsenal, their ships and landing-stages, their beloved St. Mark, their ducal palace, Rialto, harbour, moneychangers, profits, banks and trafficking. But the finest moment is undoubtedly when these old

108-109 On the third Sunday in July Venetians celebrate the Feast of the Redeemer (Il Redentore) in grand style. This is a very old tradition, dating back to the end of the plague of 1576, when the Senate of the Serenissima decided to build the church of Il Redentore in the Giudecca as a thanks offering for the city's deliverance. Pilgrims stream across a bridge of boats connecting Fondamenta delle Zattere to the splendid Palladian church. But the real festivities take place the previous evening when spectacular fireworks turn the lagoon into a riot of colour, watched by the people of Venice from boats decorated with greenery and multi-coloured balloons.

cuckolds wed the sea, of which they are the husband and the Turk is the lover." And Voltaire wondered whether the sea, i.e., the bride, was really agreeable to the marriage, especially considering the dubitable seaworthiness of a vessel like the Bucentaur, which needed favourable weather conditions to venture beyond the lagoon. Seeing the humorous side of a paradoxical situation, Casanova maintained that a tragic accident would have made Venice the laughing stock of all Europe, with the doge's marriage at last consummated as he held his bride in an eternal embrace. The last Bucentaur was brutally vandalized and practically destroyed by the French. By shattering a symbol of the ancient splendour of Venice, they intended to teach the Serenissima a lesson. Nowadays it can only be admired in paintings, or in the few remaining fragments (or a faithful small-scale model) exhibited at the Museo Storico Navale (Maritime History Museum) at the Arsenal. Today the city turns out en masse for the Vogalunga, usually held on the Sunday following Ascension Day: all the rowing associations in Venice take part in this non-competitive regatta, and St. Mark's Basin comes alive with countless boats, in a spectacular display of colour and jubilation. There are further festivities in which all Venice participates on the eve of the third Sunday in July, the Feast of the Redeemer (Il Redentore). A temporary bridge of boats is stretched across the canal to Giudecca, offering easy access to the splendid Palladian church of Il Redentore, built in thanks for the end of the terrible plague of 1576. During the night, boats decorated with greenery and picturesque lanterns crowd the canal awaiting the start of a fireworks display. A party atmosphere pervades the whole island of Giudecca; tables are set up along the length of the quayside and all the local people sit eating and drinking together. After the fireworks the boats slowly make for the Lido, where they await the sunrise. For oarsmen and Venetians at large the year's major boating event is the Historic Regatta (*Regata Storica*), held on the first Sunday in September. The entire Grand Canal is decked with flags and banners. Each palace contributes to the colourful scene and festive mood by decorating its façade with hangings and heraldic insignia. A stately procession of boats with people in period costume — intended to commemorate the arrival in Venice of the queen of Cyprus, Caterina Cornaro — travels the length of the canal, to a jubilant reception from waving crowds gathered in boats, at windows, on roof terraces and on the huge pontoon

where the jury and city authorities are seated. Then come the races and, given the Venetians' enthusiasm for this traditional event, there is no shortage of contestants. Six different categories of boats and rowers compete: gondola, *gondolina* (rowed by champions), *pupparino* (two oars, rowed by 14- to 17-year-olds), *caorlina* (six oars, manned by representatives of the different *sestieri*), *mascareta* (two oars, rowed by women) and *sandolo* (small, flat-bottomed boat). At this point a short digression to describe the boat traditionally used on the Venice lagoon — the gondola — seems appropriate. Numerous great artists have succumbed to the romantic appeal of the gondola, and it makes frequent appearances in the many travel books written about Venice. Casanova transformed it into a secret bedchamber for his passionate encounters. Goethe, in his *Epigrams*, refers to the gondola when considering the strange dualism of Life and Death: he sees it as a cradle, an image of life, in which the passenger is gently rocked and soothed, while the *felze* (the hard top covering the central part of the gondola) is a spacious, comfortable coffin. Wagner associates it with nocturnal serenades and moments of silence interspersed by the rhythmic, musical strokes of the oars and the gentle splash heard as the vessel skims gracefully over the water. Since time immemorial the gondola has been surrounded by its own special charm and magic. Its very name is an etymological mystery, adrift amid disputed Greek,

110-111 Another festivity in which the whole city participates is the Historic Regatta (Regata Storica), a celebration of rowing skills held on the first Sunday in September. The event is preceded by a grand procession of boats, that winds its way the whole length of the Grand Canal. The procession is intended to recall the historic return to Venice, in 1489, of Caterina Cornaro, widow of James of Lusignan and queen of Cyprus, who donated her precious realm to the Serenissima.

Latin, Byzantine or Illyrian origins. Its black lopsided form speeds effortlessly through the canals, skimming over the water with an elegance that continues to inspire new images, new emotions. A romantic legend traces its birth to a bright crescent moon that plunged into the sea rather than shine indiscreetly on the passionate embrace of two young lovers. Its black colour came about when the luminous glow of the moon's metallic body was suddenly extinguished by the chilly waters of the lagoon. But the gleaming metal at each end of the gondola — the pronged *ferro* on the prow and the curved one on the stern — is seen as testimony to the sparkling moon. Gondola and lyricism are destined to be eternally entwined. The body of the gondola is made from wood — a warm, vibrant material — and in Venice there are still master shipwrights who can turn timbers into vessels of outstanding elegance and technical perfection. These craftsmen work in the last remaining *squeri,* small boatbuilding yards where gondolas and other crafts are made. In recent years they have benefited from the renewed interest in Venetian-style rowing (i.e., in a standing position), which has given a new lease on life to many rowing clubs. A close look at a *forcola* (oar lock) tells you that the skilled hands of these craftsmen can

produce a work of art: carved from a single block of burled walnut, this part of the gondola is a wood sculpture in which each sharp edge and smooth curve has a precise function when manoeuvring the oar. Making gondolas is more than a tradition: it is a ritual that elevates rowing virtually to an artform, celebrated in the *squeri* of Venice for over a thousand years. At one time there were many such places in the city, scattered along all the main canals and embankments. They were divided into two categories: *da grosso* where vessels of intermediate or large tonnage were made, and *da sotil*, for gondolas and flat-bottomed boats. But here, as in every other respect, life in Venice has changed: no longer does the city have an army of sawyers, joiners and caulkers, in other words, carpenters each with their own specific field of competence, respectively cutting and preparing wood, constructing vessels or stopping their seams and making them watertight. Today the skilled hands capable of working such miracles belong to just a few men, now well on in years. They are trying, not without problems, to leave the precious legacy implicit in their trade to a younger generation, in the hope of ensuring a future for this once precious and fundamental activity. Our overview of Venetian festivities has

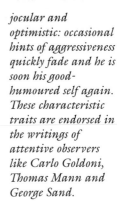

112-113 With its sinuous, elegant curves and asymmetrical shape, the gondola is the Venetian boat par excellence. As is evident from paintings by Carpaccio, Tintoretto and Canaletto, its form changed slightly through the centuries but since the 1700s it has remained as we see it today. A traditional feature of the gondola is the skilfully crafted metal ferro, with its intriguing prongs on the prow: legend has it that its shape symbolizes the bend in the Grand Canal and the six sestieri into which Venice is divided. The ferro on the stern is said to represent the island of Giudecca. Wearing his "uniform" of straw hat, striped shirt and white trousers, the gondolier is an intrinsic part of his black-varnished craft which — in a symbolic dualism of life and death — has inspired generations of poets and writers. He knows the most intimate secrets of the gondola, which he manoeuvres with amazing agility and grace. By nature he is essentially jocular and optimistic: occasional hints of aggressiveness quickly fade and he is soon his good-humoured self again. These characteristic traits are endorsed in the writings of attentive observers like Carlo Goldoni, Thomas Mann and George Sand.

114-115 Depicted in this photo is the Molo, with snow-covered gondolas bound together to mooring poles of the landing area most used by tourists. It is an ideal way to explore the city on foot and discover how a change of apparel can enhance the charm of Venice.

Winter, too, reveals her dual nature. Occasionally she abandons the slothful mood typical of the quiet, drowsy season and sends high winds — the celebrated bora — sweeping across the lagoon, blowing like the devil into every nook and cranny.

116-117 Squero is the Venetian word for a gondola building yard. It derives from the Italian term squadra *(the try square used by carpenters and joiners). This picturesque* squero *at San Trovaso is still functioning today, and all kinds of boats but particularly gondolas are made there. Timber to build gondolas has to be selected by a master craftsman and no fewer than eight different types of wood are needed: fir, larch, cherry, walnut, elm, oak, lime and mahogany. In the old days the*

ferro *on the prow and stern of the gondola were made from ductile iron by specialized craftsmen in Maniago and Forno di Zoldo; nowadays they are mass-produced in a small factory near Marghera.*

116

almost reached its end. The last important date in the calendar is in autumn, November 21, when Venice celebrates the Madonna della Salute. The focal point of this essentially religious event is the church designed by Longhena, a grand edifice built as a thanksgiving for deliverance from the devastating plague of 1630, described in all its drama by Manzoni in *The Betrothed*. Pilgrims make their way in procession across a bridge of boats to worship in the church dedicated to St. Maria della Salute, the Virgin of Health and Salvation. This too is a religious festival, in a city traditionally marked by a profound dichotomy between the sacred and profane. Throughout history religion was emphatically present in all aspects of Venetian life. But so was the awareness that the State took priority over the Church, and here the State was the Serenissima, the city itself. Pious devotion or profane love? There could be no finer response than Titian's: born in Cadore but Venetian by adoption, he was one of the few artists able to switch from the vibrant, pagan sensuality of Venus to a majestic, spiritually moving Assumption (in the Frari Church in Venice), immortalizing both with the magical use of colour that was his trademark.

THE ISLANDS OF
THE LAGOON

The Venice Lagoon is dotted with a myriad of tiny islands: over the centuries some have disappeared while others have been altered beyond recognition by changes to the lagoon environment, mostly the doing of man. Venice herself comprises over a hundred islands, big and small; the city is crossed by about 150 canals and *rii* and some 400 bridges connect each islet to its neighbour. Also situated in the lagoon — close to an urban conglomeration which is not unlike an enormous jigsaw puzzle formed of countless tiny pieces — are about 70 named islands, only few of them included on traditional tourist itineraries. Directly opposite St. Mark's Square is the island of San Giorgio Maggiore, once known as the island of cypress trees. Its predominating feature is the splendid Benedictine monastery complex, with its church (by Andrea Palladio), a bell-tower affording a marvellous view of the lagoon, and the monastery itself, since 1951 occupied by the prestigious Fondazione Giorgio Cini, still the most important cultural centre in Venice; it was established by count Vittorio Cini and named after his son. Situated close to San Giorgio, moving southwest, is Giudecca. The island was originally called Spinalonga, since its elongated shape vaguely resembles a fish bone (*spina*); its present name probably stems from the first Jewish community established in

the city, before the existing ghetto, although a number of scholars trace the name's origin to the word *zudegà*, meaning *res judicata* and applied to land allotted by a judgment to certain dissentient families banished from Venice. The many splendid patrician palaces with vegetable gardens and vineyards were ousted at the end of the nineteenth century to make way for factories, and much of the island has since been given over to working-class housing. In July the island dons its most festive mood and attire for the religious feast-day of the Redeemer: colourful celebrations on the eve, a procession across a bridge of boats linking the island to Venice proper and the culminating visit to the church of Il Redentore, one of Palladio's finest works. The island of Venice Lido acquired celebrity status in far more recent times. In the early 1920s, in his delightful guide *L'ame de Venice*, Henri Gambier painted this flattering picture: "A large town with luxurious villas, where gardens refreshed by jets from numerous fountains are always in flower; a splendid beach, palatial buildings, bathing establishments, beach cabins by the thousand; wide, shady avenues, and many streets where each house has a garden. All the amenities of city life: abundant transport, cars, trams, as well as motorboats and gondolas in the canals; electric street lamps, and a wealth of illumination. This is what

118 The island of San Giorgio Maggiore in St. Mark's Basin presents a striking picture, with its Palladian church, tall campanile and two beacon-towers in Istrian stone. Since 1951 its buildings have housed the Fondazione Giorgio Cini, with its internationally esteemed cultural studies centre.

119 The narrow, elongated shape of Giudecca — clearly visible in this aerial view — explains the island's earliest name: Spinalonga. Once resplendent with vegetable gardens and vineyards and grand patrician residences, Giudecca changed drastically at the end of the 19th century when factories and tenement housing for workers took over large areas. The island comes to life in July, with the famed celebrations on the eve of the Feast of the Redeemer.

120 top Today Venice Lido is one of the most famous beach resorts of the entire Adriatic; as well as typical tourist attractions, it has some fine examples of Art Nouveau and Art Deco architecture.

120-121 San Lazzaro degli Armeni. The Serenissima often relied on Armenian merchants to procure supplies in the East. This helps explain the decision, in 1717, to grant perpetual occupancy of the island of San Lazzaro to the Armenian priest, Mechitar, then in search of asylum (the island was named after Lazurus because of a previous leper hospital on the site). After a print shop was installed here in 1789, this lively community of Mechitarist monks became a major centre of culture and learning.

the Lido offers as a city." This was the Lido in its heyday, when international high society had fallen for the island's charms: its delights had first been extolled by Lord Byron, who wrote romantic descriptions of bathing and horseback riding, at a time when the Lido was still a desolate tract of land with few houses and inhabitants; as the subsequent paradise of earthly pleasures frequented by the beau monde, it was immortalized in the writings of Thomas Mann. Separated from Venice by a short stretch of the lagoon, the island can be reached by gondola or on the (relatively) faster water-buses which, in now distant days, carried international aristocracy across the water to a miniature Eden where Art Nouveau architecture provided a superb backdrop to the summertime activity in vogue among the resort's glitterati: sea-bathing. The idea first came to a foresighted entrepreneur called Giovanni Busetto, nicknamed Fisola, who in 1857 set up his first bathing establishment with 50 cabins. From small beginnings his venture ballooned; in the first decade of the century the Hotel des Bains was built, followed by the Excelsior Palace Hotel. To present-day visitors the Lido offers more than one of the loveliest beaches of the Adriatic: it is also a delightful compendium of the lagoon's Art Nouveau architecture — exemplified by villas like Mon Plaisir, in Viennese Secession style, designed by architect Guido Sullam in 1904–1905 — skilfully set in a verdant natural scenario. These are surely the most important islands of the lagoon, but three others have far greater tourist appeal: Murano, mecca of glasswares, Burano, renowned for its lace, and Torcello, cradle of art. Murano lies nearest to Venice, just a short ride by water-bus from Fondamente Nuove. In spite of its closeness and intense trade relations with Venice, it was granted some exceptional privileges by its powerful neighbour: these included a local government, its own statutes and even its own Podestà and Greater and Lesser Councils. It even had its own Golden Book, in which names of families with special privileges were inscribed. The somewhat atypical qualities of its population are described by the abbot Vincenzo Zanetti — in the unambiguous terms one might expect from a preacher — in his *Concise Guide* to the island: "Wishing to speak of the character of the islanders of Murano, it must be said that they are vehement enemies of indolence and sloth; by nature they are intelligent, industrious and hardworking, warmhearted and hospitable in the extreme, somewhat inclined to extravagance, although some individuals of a temperate and thrifty bent are undoubtedly to be found amongst them. Certain aspects of their personality reflect the nature of the fire and glass with which they spend practically their

121 top In 1857
Giovanni Busetto,
nicknamed Fisola —
a man with a nose
for business —
opened the first
bathing
establishment on
the island of Lido

di Venezia.
His notable success
led to further
initiatives: in the
early 1900s the Hôtel
des Bains was built,
followed by the
Excelsior Palace
Hotel.

122-123 Founded by people fleeing from Altino during the Lombard invasion, Murano was first called Amurianum, after one of the gates of their city. It has been famous for centuries as the cradle of the art of glassmaking.

122 bottom and 123 top Through the centuries the glassmakers of Murano have perfected their art, and precious examples of ever-improved wares can be admired in Palazzo Giustinian, home of the island's Glass Museum.

123 bottom Thanks to its fragility and lightness, blown glass can materialize in countless forms: filigree, aventurine, murrine (jewellery), milky white latticino, coloured glasswares. New products and styles have been introduced, in some cases the work of acclaimed 20th-century designers and artists.

entire lives: their fiery, spirited disposition and their unstable, short-lived resolutions. The plague afflicts so many cities — forcing hordes of depraved youths into the eager embrace of idleness — has made no appearance in Murano, where boys are set to work in the glasshouses at even too early an age." In their respective ways this monk and Antonio Salviati were instigators of the revival of Murano and its glassmaking activity. In the nineteenth century it fell on hard times, with few orders and the flow of tourists reduced to a mere trickle. By then Bohemian crystal and Limoges porcelain had ousted the fine-quality handcrafted glasswares made for centuries in Murano. But today "red" Murano has nothing to fear: it is high on the list of destinations selected by package tour operators. Its glass factories may suffer occasional setbacks, but these are attributable to the price and not the quality of its products, undoubtedly superior to the glasswares churned out in Hong Kong and China, manufacturing centres that dearly would like to turn the tables and snatch a significant share of the market from the new descendants of Marco Polo. Murano glass is unique: it imprisons the colours of this magical island, it pulsates with the warm gusts of the southeast wind. From soft, wet silica sand, mixed with lime and fused with the aid of soda, it acquires the vigour and strength of the lagoon's fiery sunsets. Have you ever seen the extraordinary explosion of colour that sets the lagoon aflame before the deadening shadows of night descend or with the very first light of the new day? It is at moments like these that Venice explains to mere humans why the palette of its artists has only one range of colours (in a city like Venice there is bound to be a good reason). Only poets can find appropriate words to describe the spectacle witnessed as the twilight glow turns the heavens to deepest purple. It is an awe-inspiring sight, immortalized by Gabriele D'Annunzio in his most celebrated novel. All Venice is ablaze, her buildings profiled in dark contrast to the sky. And, with her last glowing rays, the sun sinks slowly into the lagoon, a fitting reminder of the splendours of the city's glorious past. As though by magic Murano glass has captured this strength, these colours, the dazzling brilliance of the setting sun and the first gentle light of dawn. The best place to see how a raw material of such simplicity can be graced with such elegant form is in one of the many glasshouses along the Rio dei Vetrai or in Murano's Museo Vetrario (Glass Museum), the island's main attraction. The objects displayed there are truly magnificent. Housed since 1861, at the initiative of abbot Zanetti, in Palazzo Giustinian, this precious collection chronicles the evolution of glassmaking, from the very earliest archaeological finds to glass products of the present day. The exhibits span from ancient glass artifacts of Alexandria, Syria and Rome to the Venetian Renaissance, crowned by a late fifteenth-century dark blue Barovier marriage cup, a splendid —

and much copied — masterpiece, enameled with allegories of youth (the Fountain of Love and the Cavalcade) and delightful portraits of the bride and groom. Many items formerly preserved in the Correr Museum in Venice were added to these collections after the administrative functions of the municipalities of Venice and Murano were merged. The outcome is a unique selection of priceless glasswares: goblets with delicate stems, chandeliers, flasks decorated with aristocratic coats of arms or beautiful boat-shaped jugs (one exhibited in the museum was made by Armenia Vivarini in the first half of the sixteenth century).

In the eighteenth century, Bohemian glasshouses offered serious competition, but Murano added an almost ethereal lightness to its creations: opaline glass fruit stands, wares made from chalcedony or *latticino*, a milky white glass; carafes and glasses decorated with polychrome enamel or embellished with threads of gold filigree; chandeliers with exquisite floral ornamentation; mirrors set in delicately engraved frames with bold patterns in the middle. These splendid collections continue through the centuries to reach the refined elegance of Art Nouveau, and the outstanding

products of modern design. Nowhere as in Murano do we realize that glass is a timeless material of unequalled charm and beauty, able to satisfy the aesthetic tastes of the most demanding public, a product outside the reach of fads and fashions. Murano is the home of glass. Burano is, on the other hand, a small-scale Venice, with canals, alleys, and fishermen's cottages painted in triumphant colours that seem to vary according to the season and viewpoint. It is a delightful island, characterized by tiny passageways, houses with ogival arches, narrow quaysides piled with fishing nets laid out to dry in the sun. Inhabited by fishermen who speak a melodious dialect, it was the birthplace of the composer Baldassarre Galuppi, known as Il Buranello. Burano is deservedly world-famous for its lace, the celebrated *punto in aria* (the earliest type of needlepoint): talented fingers using only needle and thread turn this entirely "free" lace into incredibly beautiful embroidery. And it is not surprising to learn that the history of this lace is inextricably entwined with a mythical tale of adventures on the high seas. A young man of Burano — so the legend goes — betrothed to a beautiful young girl of the island, was forced to leave his

beloved island in search of work, and set sail for the distant Orient. After crossing many seas, his ship reached an ocean where the waters swarmed with enticing Sirens. Like Ulysses before them, all the other sailors bound one another to the ship's masts to avoid falling into the water and, above all, succumbing to the mermaids with their bewitching songs. But our young man from Burano — fired by undying love for his future bride — did not fall prey to their charms. Exceedingly impressed — and, we might add, just a little piqued by his unyielding faithfulness — the queen of the mermaids asked to meet him. Touched by his innocence, she offered him a precious gift: swishing her tail against the ship's side, she stirred up a soft mass of foam that, in her hands, turned into a lovely bridal veil. When inventing a tale to explain the origins of beautiful handiwork that appears to have been produced with a touch of magic, human imagination is boundless. The exhibits at the Museo del Merletto (Lace Museum), adjoining the old, centrally located Palazzo del Podestà, make visitors realize that only a myth could adequately account for the skill and dedication of Burano's lace-makers. Burano is renowned for its colour

as well as its lace. Painters chose the island as the venue for a prestigious art prize, now called the *Premio di pittura Burano*. The world of art and artists still pervades Romano Barbaro's celebrated tavern where the walls are literally covered in paintings, watercolours, drawings and extraordinary caricatures bearing the names of Pio Semeghini, Filippo De Pisis, Gino Rossi and numerous other artists who have drawn inspiration from this island and its colours. The painters who founded a colony here intended to turn their backs on the Venice Biennale (on bitter memories of rejected works) and on conventional lagoon artistry, considered veduta painting at its most stereotypical. Torcello is the last island on our itinerary. The silence that reigns here is proverbial, as are its great, empty stretches of meadowland. It is hard to believe this small island was once inhabited by the people of Altino on the Italian mainland, who fled their homes after barbarian plunderers totally destroyed this ancient Roman settlement. Legend often fills gaps left by chroniclers of antiquity and, in the history of this island, fact has been embellished by fantasy. According to a story passed down through the centuries, the people of Altino

128-129 Peace and quiet reign on the island of San Francesco del Deserto, inhabited only by Franciscan monks. Situated between Sant'Erasmo and Burano, the island occupies an area of almost 5 acres and, with the tall cypresses framing its church and monastery, it is an ideal place for prayer and meditation. According to tradition, in 1220 St. Francis of Assisi himself came to stay on this pleasant island in the Venice lagoon.

128 bottom A visit to Torcello is not to be missed by lovers of history and particularly of the period when Venice was first starting to develop. In this outpost of the lagoon's civilization, with its tranquil atmosphere and green surroundings, the historic landmarks are the cathedral of Santa Maria Assunta, with the splendid mosaic of the Last Judgement, *the church of Santa Fosca and the legendary throne of Attila.*

129 bottom Venice lagoon is dotted with tiny, once inhabited islands used through the centuries as lazarettos, gunpowder stores and monasteries. Some have completely disappeared; others are mere sandbanks again, emerging at low tide and visited only by birds, their surfaces continuously eroded by the powerful ebbs and flows of the lagoon.

had a premonition of an impending Lombard invasion; powerless to stop the barbarian hordes, they implored divine intervention. The flight of a flock of birds, abandoning their nests with their young, was interpreted as a sign from God and the people fled, some towards Istria, others to the Byzantine city of Ravenna; others put their trust in a voice from heaven that (in good ecclesiastical Latin, language of the Holy Mother Church) announced, "*In turrem ascendite, ab astra autem videte.*" As instructed, they climbed to the top of a tower and saw the island in the lagoon that was destined to be their place of refuge. They named their new settlement Turris or Turricellum, now Torcello, after the tower they had climbed in their native city. The present population of this island is now totally dependent on tourism for its survival, but there was once — so history books tell us — a thriving city of 20,000 people, a seat of local government and a bishopric. The sole remaining testimonies to its splendid past are to be seen in the square: the so-called Attila's seat (actually used by the tribunes responsible for upholding justice) and the fourteenth-century palaces of the Council and the Archives. These buildings

now house Torcello's Museum, with its important collections of archaeological exhibits from Roman, Early Christian and medieval times. The religious sentiment of those days can still be sensed in the church of Santa Fosca, with its distinctive portico, and in the Cathedral of Santa Maria Assunta, founded — as an ancient epigraph conserved in the basilica reveals — in far-off 639, by order of Isacio, exarch of Ravenna. The Venetian-Byzantine mosaics (the *Last Judgement*, plus a *Madonna and Child* in the apse) are breathtakingly beautiful and, as the light catches their dazzling colours, the whole church is transformed by the splendour. These descriptions and pictures are an attempt to capture and convey the unique charm and magic of Venice, a city suffused with a fascination that can never fade, "the fairy city of my heart," as George Gordon Byron called it in *Childe Harold's Pilgrimage*. Mystery remains the key to the magic of Venice, from the city's earliest origins to its as yet unknown — and no less mysterious — future, spanning centuries during which Venice has reaped the precious legacy of her past and captivated hearts with the aid of benevolent deities.

130-131 Colour is the trademark of the island and the buranelli, *with the canniness typical of fishing folk, have inherited the talent to make the very most of the changing hues of the lagoon, drawing writers and especially painters, into their magical web. As the observant poet Diego Valeri writes in his delightful* Fantasie veneziane: *"Artists come here, from Venice or Milan. They look out over the Terranova canal and instantly note the effects of contrasting and complementary shades, alternating highs and lows, upbeats and downbeats. And they gaze in wonder at this interplay, so masterly yet so totally natural."*

136 Aerial view of Venice.

INDEX

BIBLIOGRAPHY

Introduction
(1) I. Brodskij, *Fondamenta degli Incurabili*, Venice 1991, pages 17-18.
(2) M. Barrès, *La Morte di Venezia*, Milan 1926, pages 56-57.

Monumental Venice: Historic Sites and Museums
(1) D. Valeri, *Guida Sentimentale di Venezia*, Padova, 1942, pages 44-45.
(2) G. Casanova, *Storia della mia fuga dalle prigioni di Venezia dette Piombi*, Milan, 1911.
(3) *La Cena in casa di Levi di Paolo Veronese*, Vicenza, 1965.
(4) A. Sarfatti, *Rime veneziane*, Venice, 1884, pages 49-52.

Exploring Venice
(1) I. Montanelli, *Com'è difficile salvare Venezia*, Corriere della Sera November 22, 1995.
(2) T. Marinetti, *Sintesi del Futurismo*, Rome, 1968, pages 15-16.

(3) P. de Commynes, *Memorie*, Turin, 1960.
(4) W. Goethe, *Viaggio in Italia*, Florence, 1924, Vol. I, page 97.
(5) Thomas Mann, *Death in Venice*, Milan, 1959, pages 82-83.
(6) Dante Alighieri, *Divine Comedy*, Inferno, XXI, VV. 7-18.

Carnival and Traditional Venetian Festivities
(1) J. Lecomte, *Venise...*, Paris, 1844, page 36.
(2) J. Du Bellay, *Regrets*, 1558, CXXXIII.

The Islands of the Lagoon
(1) H. Gambier, *L'âme de Venise*, Paris, 1921, pages 127-128.
(2) V. Zanetti, *Piccola guida di Murano*, Venice, 1869, page 25.
(3) D. Valeri, *Fantasie veneziane*, Milan, 1972, page 87.